1987

CONVENTIONS
&CHOICES

———— ♦ ————

*A Brief Book of Style
and Usage*

CONVENTIONS & CHOICES

———— ♦ ————

A Brief Book of Style and Usage

STEPHEN MERRIAM FOLEY
Brown University

JOSEPH WAYNE GORDON
Yale University

D. C. HEATH AND COMPANY
Lexington, Massachusetts   Toronto

Acquisition Editor: Paul Smith
Project Editor: Holt Johnson
Production Editor: Rosemary Rodensky
Designer: Sally Steele

Published simultaneously in Canada.

Printed in the United States of America.

International Standard Book Number: 0-669-07544-2

Library of Congress Catalog Card Number: 85-80168

USING THIS BOOK

♦

We have addressed this book to all writers, but especially to those who take the time to write more than one draft of their work. We assume that in writing these drafts, you are not just looking for errors, but examining the consequences of decisions that you have made, thoughtfully or inadvertently, in the process of writing. We have tried to point out the places in the composing process at which there are decisions to make and to offer writers who are facing these decisions the grounds for intelligent choice.

While every writer has to make many decisions, these decisions do not have to be made either all at once or once and for all. Postponing some of them or regarding them as temporary can keep open the possibility of making substantive new discoveries. Even up to the last minute, a writer is always getting started. Exploratory procedures like making lists, drawing upon free association, reading and researching, mapping, daydreaming, or consulting a handbook may be appropriate at any stage in the composing process.

But if writers are in some ways always getting started, they are also always rewriting. Rewriting is more than just going back and scratching out or filling in. It is a means of going forward. Rewriting should involve posing new, cogent questions as well as settling old ones. It can mean exploring new directions as well as finding the way back from digressions.

This book is set up to help you throughout the writing process. It will permit both the leisurely browsing helpful when you are trying to get started on a writing project and the quick reference necessary when you are hurrying to finish the project. It should help to resolve the problems that you recognize and lead you to recognize others that you may have overlooked. The first part, *Organizing the Writing Process,* explains the importance of conventions to the writer's work. It offers advice on selecting evidence and on determining when and how to form paragraphs. The second part, *Syntax and Structure,* discusses matters ranging from the construction of sentences to the function of pronouns. The third part, *Diction and Usage,* begins with an essay that explores historical changes in the meaning of words and describes the appropriate and inappropriate uses of some familiar phrases. The alphabetical glossary following the essay calls attention to words and phrases often misused and either suggests better uses for these words or better words for these uses. The fourth part deals with manuscript preparation. It examines common punctuation marks, some fundamental matters of typography such as the use of capital letters and italics, and the formation of possessives. It concludes with examples and guidelines for documentation of sources.

Like all writers, we are grateful to readers whose timely advice has saved us from being trapped in our own first draft. At its best, revision is a communal labor, and we are truly indebted to the friends, colleagues, and students who generously offered their help, especially to Marie Borroff, Joseph Germano, Nicholas Howe, Dominic Kinsley, Elaine Maimon, Louis Martz, Clarence Miller, Fred Robinson, and Robert Scholes. We also acknowledge with thanks the criticism offered by our no longer anonymous readers for D. C. Heath: Jo Ann Bomze, Michael Gustin, Gerald Mulderig, and Thomas Toon. Paul Smith, our Acquisition Editor at D. C. Heath, Holt Johnson, our Project Editor, and Rosemary Rodensky, who copyedited our manuscript with intelligence and care, deserve our special thanks and praise for their efforts on our behalf. And we are grateful to Mary Jo Foley for having helped us see our book through from the very beginning.

S.M.F.
J.W.G.

CONTENTS

———— ♦ ————

/ 2 3, 7 6 6

PART I

---◆---

ORGANIZING
THE PROCESS
OF WRITING

Convention and Organization

— ♦ —

Writing and Convention

Whether language brings thought or thought brings language, even the first words that come to a writer seem to fit into patterns. Some of these patterns may stem from the writer's own habits of mind, but many of them are influenced by the practices and procedures of an established community of writers and readers. Any occasion for writing calls forth from the writer certain turns of phrase, tones of voice, and modes of argument. These phrases, voices, and arguments will define the occasion of the writing to the reader. Our whole experience of writing and reading builds the ability to produce and recognize these conventional patterns, and conventions guide almost every choice we have to make in the process of composing.

Conventions also affect the ways in which writers open their work to their readers' interpretation. Lawyers and novelists both seek to control the inferences that the reader makes from their writing, but the sort of ambiguity that fascinates the reader of fiction is not the same as that which makes for interesting litigation over a contract. Whether a community of writers comprises all the members of a single profession or just those students present in a single classroom at a particular time, its conventional practices determine not just how issues can be resolved, but how they cannot.

Some conventions guide matters of scope, specificity, and the relative importance of information. The ways in which a journalist and a scientist report the discovery and cloning of intact human genetic material from an Egyptian mummy, for example, differ not just in the use they make of the technical vocabulary of biochemistry or in the length and rhythm of their sentences, but in the authority they accord to different data. The scientist, writing in *Nature,* a scientific journal, narrows his argument for the scrutiny of the scientific community:

> Artificial mummification was practised in Egypt from ~ 2600 BC until the fourth century AD. Because of the dry Egyptian climate, however, there are also many natural mummies preserved from earlier as well as later times. To elucidate whether this unique source of ancient human remains can be used for molecular genetic analyses, 23 mummies were investigated for DNA content. One 2,400-yr-old mummy of a child was found to contain DNA that could be molecularly cloned in a plasmid vector. I report here that one such clone contains two members of the *Alu* family of human repetitive DNA sequences, as detected by DNA hybridizations and nucleotide sequencing. These analyses show that substantial pieces of mummy DNA (3.4 kilobases) can be cloned and that the DNA fragments seem to contain little or no modifications introduced postmortem.
>
> *Nature,* 314:6012 (April 18–24, 1985).

The *New York Times* reporter, basing his article on the report in *Nature,* presents the biologist's claims as an important and fascinating scientific accomplishment:

> Human genetic material, largely undamaged after 2,400 years, has been extracted from an Egyptian

mummy and has been grown in the laboratory. The achievement is the most dramatic of a series of recent accomplishments using molecular biology to study links between modern and ancient life.

New York Times (April 16, 1985).

Students of every subject, trying to make their prose read like that of experts, are sometimes first-rate, if unconscious, mimics of the conventional practices of professional writers. And with good reason, since the conventions of writing define the professions and differentiate among the academic disciplines in little ways as well as big ones. Sociologists, who classify and name patterns of social behavior, tend to string together long phrases of nouns. In "The Culture of Poverty," Oscar Lewis writes:

> The disengagement, the nonintegration, of the poor with respect to the major institutions of society is a crucial element in the culture of poverty. It reflects the combined effect of a variety of factors including poverty, to begin with, but also segregation and discrimination, fear, suspicion and apathy and the development of alternative institutions and procedures in the slum community.

Historians, who are given more to the narration and analysis of actions, rely on verbs. Barbara Tuchman shows this style in *A Distant Mirror:*

> When the plague entered northern France in July 1348, it settled first in Normandy and, checked by winter, gave Picardy a deceptive interim until the next summer. Either in mourning or warning, black flags were flown from church towers of the worst-stricken villages of Normandy. "And in that time," wrote a monk of the abbey of Fourcarment, "the mortality was so great among the people of Normandy that those of Picardy mocked them." The same unneighborly reaction was reported of the Scots, separated by a winter's immunity from the English. Delighted to hear of the disease that was scourging the "southrons," they gathered forces

for an invasion, "laughing at their enemies." Before they could move, the savage mortality fell upon them too, scattering some in death and the rest in panic to spread the infection as they fled.

Unlike experimental psychologists, clinical psychologists conventionally make use of the pronoun *I* in their reports. The two branches of this community of writers differ in how they demonstrate objectivity or impartiality in their prose. Consider, for example, the difference between these two excerpts. The first, by Bruno Bettelheim, is from *Scientific American;* the second, by Stanley Milgram, is from *Human Relations.*

Joey's mother impressed us with a fey quality that expressed her insecurity, her detachment from the world and her low physical vitality. We were struck especially by her total indifference as she talked about Joey. This seemed much more remarkable than the actual mistakes she made in handling him. Certainly he was left to cry for hours when hungry, because she fed him on a rigid schedule; he was toilet-trained with great rigidity so that he would give no trouble. These things happen to many children. But Joey's existence never registered with his mother. In her recollections he was fused at one moment with one event or person; at another, with something or somebody else. When she told us about his birth and infancy, it was as if she were talking about some vague acquaintance, and soon her thoughts would wander off to another person or to herself.

The focus of the study concerns the amount of electric shock a subject is willing to administer to another person when ordered by an experimenter to give the "victim" increasingly more severe punishment. The act of administering shock is set in the context of a learning experiment, ostensibly designed to study the effect of punishment on memory. Aside from the experimenter, one naïve subject and one accomplice perform in each session. On arrival each subject is paid $4.50. After a general talk by the experimenter, telling how little scientists know about the effect of punishment on memory, subjects are informed that one member of the pair will serve as teacher and one as learner. A rigged drawing is held so that the naïve subject is always the teacher, and the accomplice becomes the learner. The learner is taken to an adjacent room and strapped into an "electric chair."

The goal of learning the conventions of any professional or intellectual community is to prompt invention, not imitation. For while the existence of conventions shows that no occasion for writing is unique, each occasion is distinctive—even a series of assignments that look superficially alike. Well-read, experienced writers welcome the help that conventional approaches offer, but are always wary of the danger of mistaking the problem at hand for a simpler, more usual one. Conventions will help to point out what is already known about approaching the problem. It is up to the writer to use this knowledge to discover what more can be said or, rather, written.

At times, in fact, a sophisticated writer will deliberately write against the conventions. To question fundamental assumptions, to redefine the terms of debate, perhaps just to startle readers whose expectations have become too fixed, a writer must violate (not ignore) conventional standards or practices in a profession or field of study. The following paragraph, from William Ryan's *Planning Our Vacation*, mocks the social scientist's penchant for long noun phrases and acronyms:

> Academic and political experts on poverty and the poor have given wide currency to the proposition that this distribution is highly related to social class position. The pattern of behavior characterized by ability to delay need-gratification—what has been called the Deferred Gratification Pattern (D.G.P.)—is supposedly characteristic of the middle classes. Members of the lower classes, in contrast, are usually rumored to display the Non-deferred

Gratification Pattern (N.G.P.). The formula has all the force and simplicity of a classical cigarette advertising commercial: M.C./D.G.P.; L.C./N.G.P. All it lacks is a catchy tune.

Conventions are powerful tools, but knowledge of them, whether derived from deliberate study of professional writing or from quick reference to a handbook, should guide rather than force choices. In the various sections of this book, we describe conventions of structure, syntax, usage, and punctuation and explain how they affect matters ranging from the construction of arguments to the tense of verbs. We indicate where there are decisions to be made. Even though those decisions are finally up to the writer, we hope that this book will help to get the process of deciding, and writing, started.

Organizing for the Writer

Even before you begin to write, the conventions of discourse in your profession or discipline guide your work. Knowledge of these conventions helps you to determine how the specific occasion that you have for writing and the material that you are dealing with might engage other work in the field. Thinking about that other work will get your own writing started by suggesting ways of organizing and presenting the ideas you have now. It will also prevent boring imitation. Recognizing how the present occasion for writing differs from that other work will keep you from merely repeating your own ideas or those of others.

However you get started writing—researching, jotting down words and phrases as they come, making logical inferences, drawing up lists—a crucial first step in organizing your work must be to define what problem you are going to be writing about and to whom you will be writing. A banking executive, for example, asked to write a study of the feasibility of purchasing a new computer software system, would have to decide whether to prepare a short memo in the usual company format or a full-scale report. Have there been previous feasibility studies of software systems or of similar systems? Would they serve as appropriate models for the format of this study? The executive would also have to consider what reference this study should make to the findings of the previous studies. Should the new study summarize them? Does it need to accept or dispute them? Will it contradict some of the previous work and support other findings? The executive would also try to imagine who would be reading the study. Colleagues from the research department? An immediate superior? Senior executives? What would these different readers already know about the problem? What would they expect to learn? Only after considering these questions would it make sense for the writer to look through the notes and data that had been gathered in order to determine what material in them would be suitable for this study.

Writers of academic papers go through a similar process. Is the material at hand, whether derived through research or supplied by an assignment, better suited to a short essay or to a long formal paper? What is the scope of the project? Is the intended audience made up of specialists in the field or of generally well-educated peers, like classmates? How should the paper be related to previous work on the subject? Need it acknowledge that work? Does it have to correct or extend it? Are personal observations appropriate?

In the early stages of composing, then, writers should be moving back and forth from the larger concerns of a whole field of discourse to their particular writing project. At this stage, they need to think less about what shape they will give to their sentences and more about how their work will be shaped by previous studies.

It is probably unwise, therefore, for writers to make a detailed outline before completing a draft. Such an outline is useful for showing how a finished draft is put together and can offer a map for revising it. But an outline of something unwritten is like a medieval map of the world: it might very well lead one astray or discourage discovery of unexplored approaches. It is probably also unwise at this stage to fuss over individual words or to worry about the completeness of paragraphs. While some writers find it helpful to do a little of this sort of work early, just to get themselves into the habit of precision, they risk becoming distracted from larger, still unsettled questions and may waste energy polishing phrases that they will omit from a final version.

Organizing for the Reader

Although you are almost always your own first reader and although sometimes you may be your closest reader, you should never mistake yourself for your most important reader. A page of writing may bring together a writer and a reader, but they approach and withdraw from the page in different psychological directions. The organization of your written work should not retrace all the stages you went through in the process of composing, but indicate the stages that you want your reader to go through in the process of reading.

You need not only to know your own mind, but also to imagine that of your reader. In thinking about the appropriate reader for any piece of writing, the writer has to judge what knowledge of the subject the reader might have. How, in particular, will it differ from the writer's own knowledge? The writer must also decide upon a tone of voice to use in addressing the reader. Should it be formal, like that used to address a professional colleague? Or more informal, like that used to address a friend in a letter?

Determining how the work of writing at hand fits into a field of professional or academic discourse will help you to anticipate what expectations readers will bring to your work. Even if you set out to write for just one person, such as an associate or a teacher, you should consider that person as standing for an entire community of readers. A professor of literature reads a student's analysis of a poem not just as an individual, but as a scholar. A judge reads a lawyer's brief not just as a citizen, but as a representative of the law. These writers might have to take into account the personalities of the professor and the judge, but should address those readers less in terms of their private character than in terms of their position as authorities in a field of discourse.

Getting and keeping the reader's attention is not a matter of mastering fancy tricks. It is a matter of meeting and then exceeding (or deliberately surprising) the reader's expectations of what a competent writer will do.

To gain the reader's attention, the writer must be sure to adopt the proper format. An experienced reader of lab reports, for example, expects a report to be divided into an abstract, an introduction, a section on methods and materials, a summary of results, and a discussion of conclusions. A professional reader of the opinions of tax court judges would expect different sections of an opinion to set forth findings of fact, conclusions of law, and a final judgment. The standardization of formats allows busy readers to make quick comparisons between the work at hand and other works that they know. In some fields of discourse, such as literary criticism, there is no single model, but experienced readers of work in these fields will develop a sense of what is and what is not considered an appropriate format. Knowing the format most widely considered to be standard in a field—down to small details like the form of footnotes or abbreviations—is a first step towards membership in an intellectual community. Adopting that format gives the writer a better chance of attracting and influencing readers.

Of course, whether the purpose of a piece of writing is to persuade or merely to inform, it must present evidence. The first rule of evidence is always to take the reader into account. Every community of writers and readers establishes limits to what constitutes valid evidence in the field. Evidence that might seem unreliable to an economist trying to predict economic growth could be acceptable to a social psychologist trying to determine whether consumers believed the economy were growing. Some professions like law and some disciplines like mathematics have established strict codes of evidence, while others, like advertising and history, accept a broad range of statements as evidence. But writers in all fields must present evidence that their readers will know—or will want to learn—how to interpret. You keep the attention of your readers by offering them the possibility of making interpretations, the possibility of doing intellectual work different from your own as a writer, but dependent upon it.

A writer must not lose that attention by introducing otherwise valid but irrelevant evidence. Not all the facts and not all the observations that the writer may have gathered and verified will be relevant to the work at hand—not even all those that are derived from careful research or from painstaking concentration, not even all those that are accurate or original. Some may distract the reader. Limit yourself to evidence that will help your reader to test and acknowledge your point.

You begin the process of writing, then, by organizing the project you have before you in terms of the conventions of a field of discourse. You first determine what problems are being posed and what approaches can be taken towards solving those problems. You also need to consider the potential readers of your work. What tone of voice will you use to address these readers and what evidence will you offer to persuade or inform them?

However exciting and terrifying you find starting the process of writing, you must end by presenting your reader with a finished work. Readers from all professions and backgrounds insist that your work show careful organization in every detail, from well-chosen words to correctly placed commas. When you complete a first draft, you begin to discover what you have to say. Then you must go on writing and rewriting—replacing misused words, getting sentences to fit together, setting up paragraphs—not until your writing is free from mistakes, but until it is unmistakable.

CHAPTER

2

Paragraphing

— ♦ —

Paragraphs

Much of the actual work of paragraphing follows the completion of a sketch or rough draft. Although some paragraphs need simply to be discovered, others have to be fashioned. To a degree, a paragraph is simply an arrangement of type or script that acknowledges the limits of visual attention. While there is no absolute reason to prefer short paragraphs to long, or long to short, shorter paragraphs are perhaps more appropriate to the narrow columns of a newspaper or to the simple observations of a casual letter; and longer paragraphs to books and formal reports. But the paragraphing should never make the reader squint or strain. Avoid the single-sentence and the full-page paragraph unless you intend to startle or astonish your reader.

A paragraph is also a logical unit, each one marking a stage in an argument or a shift in its emphasis. As a logical unit, each paragraph must not only be complete in itself, but also proceed out of the one that comes before it and lead into the one that comes after it. A good paragraph is both a whole and a part. It needs a structure of its own, yet must contribute to a larger design.

Writers commonly form paragraphs out of a series of related sentences by adding certain cue phrases to emphasize the specific quality of that relation: *thus, for example, finally, therefore*. These phrases are, however, often superfluous. Even a variation in the rhythm or length of a sentence in the series, or the repetition of a crucial word or phrase can convey a clear sense of transition or summary. The introduction and the conclusion of a paragraph do not require an especially heavy hand. The writer has merely to give the reader a sense of connection and closure at the appropriate moment. This paragraph ends the first chapter of Philip Rieff's *The Triumph of the Therapeutic:*

> Freud never objected to alternative therapies, if they worked. His rejection of commitment therapies derives not so much from wounded vanity at having been abandoned by favored disciples as from his belief that there were no longer extant any communities wherein men could safely reinvest their troubled emotions in the hope of higher dividends.

The first paragraph of the next chapter begins: "The higher dividends are essentially symbolic in nature."

There are perhaps as many different kinds of paragraphs as there are modes of thought. Controlled variation in the structure of paragraphs is as refreshing as variation in the length of sentences. Yet, despite this potential variety, there are a few patterns that most readers will recognize and that exasperated writers, trying to marshal their sentences into orderly paragraphs, should have among their strategies.

Direction and Chronology

Paragraphs that offer a first description of a place or a first narration of an event usually give the reader the sense of moving consistently in a single direction in space or time, as if the order of reading were comparable to the order of observing. Such descriptions may proceed either forwards or backwards, but the conventional pattern is from top to bottom, left to right, and past to present.

Cue words like *now, next, above,* and *to the right* create this illusion of order exactly, but these words become tedious with repetition, especially when they appear again and again at the beginning of sentences:

> *First* Hurston studied anthropology at Barnard.
>
> *Then* she returned to the South to gather material for a collection of folk tales, *Mules and Men.*
>
> *Later* she made extensive use of this material in her novels.

Varying the position of the cues in the sentence or subordinating the information can alleviate some of the tedium. Rely on conjunctions rather than the cue words to convey the sense of sequence or relative position, and adjust the tense or form of verbs to make the sequence clear:

> Hurston had completed her study of anthropology at Barnard when she returned to the South to gather material for a collection of folk tales, *Mules and Men.* She later made extensive use of this material in her novels.

Another version might give a different emphasis to the sequence:

> After studying anthropology at Barnard, Hurston returned to the South to gather material for a collection of folk tales, *Mules and Men.* She made extensive use of this material in her novels.

Offering specific information about place and date, if possible, would allow the reader to infer the sequence or connection:

> Hurston was graduated from Barnard in 1928, with a degree in anthropology, and returned to the South to gather material for a collection of folk tales, *Mules and Men.* The novels that she wrote in the thirties make extensive use of this material.

This one-dimensional pattern of description and narration is so familiar that skilled writers deviate from it almost as soon as they have established it. When the reader has first felt a clear orientation or continuity, a subsequent sense of disorientation or discontinuity can provoke interest. Sometimes a one-dimensional pattern will not suit the occasion. Although in medieval romances descriptions of women began with their hair and proceeded downwards to their feet, that convention—and the attitude towards the female body that it expressed—has been superseded. A contemporary look at the female, or male, body is likely to focus more intently on fewer of its areas. The analysis of processes, whether in the lab or in the kitchen, may require an account of actions which are in fact simultaneous, but which can be undertaken or supervised only one at a time, such as carving the roast and making the gravy.

Cause and Effect

The analysis of causes and effects in history, science, and law cannot usually be organized along a single axis of time or space. Here the writer does not want to create the illusion that there is a correlation between the order of events and the order in which they are read. The proper ordering is logical, not psychological. Attention to temporal sequence or relative position might even disguise an important causal connection.

A paragraph needs to defend the propositions and assertions it makes. Since meditating or investigating may turn up a broad range of evidence, not all of it corroborative, these paragraphs must consider objections and exceptions without undermining the argument, as in the following paragraph from Evelyn Hutchinson's *The Evolutionary Theater and the Ecological Play:*

> The most important of the learning processes of *Homo sapiens,* namely the acquisition of speech, is, for everyday purposes, almost complete in child-

hood. The same is probably true of most elementary skills not involving the use of the full strength of the adult body. Provided the child is intelligent in learning to hear and to speak, and in a few other less complicated things, the major function of the learning process has been accomplished, and it has not very much mattered for the survival of most societies how profoundly intelligent most of the members have been in later life. In emergencies some highly intelligent leaders are no doubt often needed, but at most the demand for intellectual activity must be very small in relation to the supply available in childhood. A certain slowly acquired experience may always be desirable, but it is usually of things showing far less complex relationships than the words of sentences. For the average man the great period of intellectual activity must be over by the end of the first decade or decade and a half of life. It is reasonable to suppose that genetic selection for intellectual ability has mainly weeded out those too dull in childhood to learn their minimal cultural responses and has operated much less significantly on adult intellectual processes.

In his opening sentence, Hutchinson carefully limits the scope of the general proposition he is arguing. Rather than assert that the most important human learning process, the acquisition of speech, is "complete in childhood," he proposes that "for everyday purposes" this learning process is "almost" complete. At first glance, these phrases may seem weak—concessions that diminish the force of his proposition. But in fact they defend the argument against two categories of objection. Objections can now be dismissed as exceptional, not "everyday" ("emergencies," for example), or trivial (the "few other less complicated things" or the "very small" demand for intellectual activity in the average adult life). Rather than undermine his argument, Hutchinson's concessions actually strengthen its claim, in the final sentence, to being "reasonable."

Conditional sentences (if *x*, then *y*; only when *x* does *y*) are also useful for making clear the limits of generalization.

To distinguish apparent evidence from true evidence, impressions from facts, negative evidence from affirmative, the writer should use constructions with conjunctions such as *but* and *although* or adverbs such as *however* and *nonetheless.* These concessions are best placed at the beginning or middle of a paragraph to allow opportunity for refuting them. It is weak to end on a note of concession. Be sure to organize the paragraph to avoid more than one or two uses of *but* and *however.* Turning and turning about dizzies the reader.

Comparison and Contrast

Paragraphs of comparison and contrast are worked along a dual axis. On one axis, there are the topics under discussion; on the other, there are the points of comparison or contrast. Consider a discussion of the use of woodwinds by Smetana and Dvořák (topics) in their chamber music, tone poems, and operas (points of comparison). The discussion could be organized into either of two basic patterns, by topics or by points of comparison.

By Topics		*By Points of Comparison*	
A. Smetana	1. chamber music	1. chamber music	A. Smetana
	2. tone poems		B. Dvořák
	3. operas	2. tone poems	A. Smetana
B. Dvořák	1. chamber music		B. Dvořák
	2. tone poems	3. operas	A. Smetana
	3. operas		B. Dvořák

The pattern to the left would emphasize the distinctiveness, or similarity, of the two composers' scoring for woodwinds under comparable circumstances. The pattern to the right would emphasize the effect of musical forms on the orchestration of these two comparable composers.

The context of the discussion would determine which pattern to choose.

The building of comparisons requires strict parallel construction within sentences, between sentences, or between paragraphs (see pages 70–73). Parallelism makes unnecessary the frequent repetition of phrases like *in contrast, by comparison,* and *similarly.* The phrase *on the other hand* by definition should be used only once in the course of a comparison.

Comparisons are sometimes purposefully uneven. If, in the example above, the purpose were not to examine Smetana and Dvořák fully, but to use Smetana's music only as a means of evaluating how individual or how traditional Dvořák's orchestration is, Smetana's music would not have to be discussed every time that Dvořák's music is mentioned. But those characteristics of Smetana's music that were brought up should be analogous to those being considered about Dvořák.

Examples

Almost all paragraphs comprise both general propositions and specific examples. While for extraordinary purposes a paragraph might be made up entirely of general propositions, like the opening paragraph of the Declaration of Independence, or mainly of details, like a paragraph in a technical manual, most shift about readily from one level of generalization to another. Readers are so accustomed to this shift that cues such as *for example, namely,* and *to be specific* are not always necessary.

There is no rule governing the proportion of examples to propositions. The paragraph should seem neither to sag from a lack of examples nor to bulge from a surfeit. However many examples a paragraph contains, the relative importance of the material within it should be made clear. While the adverbs *also, too,* and *again* extend a series or expand a category, *furthermore* and *moreover* not only amplify but also place a slightly greater degree of emphasis

19

on the new material that follows. Remember that like *however*, these adverbs cannot do the work of a conjunction and are best placed after the word that they modify: "He *also* serves who only stands and waits."

The construction *some . . . others* and *one . . . another* may be used to offer alternative examples or propositions of nearly equal emphasis or validity. Other adverbs like *particularly, especially, merely*, and *even*, when used sparingly, lend emphasis or take it away.

When writing about a complicated topic, especially in early drafts, you may find it helpful to enumerate examples and propositions according to an ascending or descending scale of importance. *First* and *second* or *next* are useful, but to go much beyond *third* may give the reader the uncomfortable feeling of reading an outline rather than a finished piece of work. For the same reason, *more important* and *most important* should be used sparingly.

Avoid the opposite fault of failing to make distinctions of emphasis. Some paragraphs never descend from the highest pitch, with a *very, extremely,* or *all* in every sentence; others never rise from the level of cautious qualification, with frequent use of *somewhat, rather, perhaps,* and *partly*.

English syntax offers many other means for establishing order and adjusting emphasis. The following paragraph from Edmund S. Morgan's *American Slavery, American Freedom* shows how verbs can be used to make such an adjustment. Morgan is summarizing the economic program of Sir William Berkeley, governor of the Colony of Virginia:

> And yet Berkeley's plans for Virginia sound a little like New England with the Puritanism left out. The settlers *must* gather in towns, where they could better protect themselves from savage enemies without and from the savage nature that lurked within them all. Only towns and cities could nourish the arts and skills that distinguished civil men from barbarians. Surrounded by paying customers, artisans *would* no

longer be tempted to relinquish their skilled callings to earn a living by tobacco. They *would* build ships so that the colony could develop its own commerce. They *would* smelt and forge iron from the mines that *would* be discovered. They *would* spin and weave cloth from the wool and linen that the farmers outside the towns would produce. For the farmers too *would* give up their addiction to tobacco and cease to be dependent on the vagaries of the tobacco market. They *would* expand corn and wheat production for export to the sugar plantations of the West Indies. Economically, if not ideologically, Berkeley was ready to try the Yankees' game, and with a fair chance of winning. After all, Virginia enjoyed a central position in North America, close to the West Indies, and close (it was then supposed) to the rich Spanish settlements on the Pacific. Virginia *should* be the center of England's New World empire.

The use of *must* in the second sentence suggests not only Berkeley's sense of the necessity of building towns, but also his prerogative as governor to bring about their construction. The repeated use of *would* throughout the middle of the paragraph conveys the insistence of Berkeley's logic— his notion that the growth of commerce and industry depends solely on the prior development of a concentrated market. *Would* here also conveys Berkeley's sense of the settlers' willingness to conform to his plans. And the climactic shift from *would* to *should* in the final sentence emphasizes the sense of mission that lies behind the governor's entire program.

Remember that paragraphing should be the concern of the writer, not the reader. Paragraphs are not prose stanzas. In following a well-developed argument or description, the reader will scarcely pause for the completion of each paragraph. One good paragraph leads to another, and the writer who controls such matters of technique will also control the argument of his work as a whole.

PART II

—— ◆ ——

SYNTAX
AND
STRUCTURE

3

Syntax and
the Process of Writing

— ♦ —

Shaping Your Writing

Syntax—not just the grammatical organization of a language, but the opportunities that the language affords for putting words together—may actually direct or redirect the process of writing. Whatever the writer is trying to express, syntax can provide several possible forms for phrases and clauses and can influence even the length and rhythm of sentences. As soon as sentences begin to take shape, the writer is inevitably involved in the game (sometimes the task) of fitting the promptings of the mind to the patterns of the language.

All the words that come to mind have meaning, but the sentences that a writer composes will limit or extend this meaning. When they are being fitted together, words may seem as if they were elements of logic, at least so far as to demand consistent or categorical treatment. Singular verbs normally have to agree with singular subjects, and plural verbs with plural subjects. The categories that English syntax supplies are among a writer's greatest resources. Marking the mood of verbs, for example, quickly

25

distinguishes real conditions (indicative mood) from hypothetical ones (subjunctive mood), and marking the tense differentiates present actions from those in the past or future.

Groups of words can also act as if they have mass or dimension and thereby dispose writers to think of the sentence as a structure. In building these structures, writers must place related words together to support one another. Phrases and modifiers that dangle off either end of the sentence may threaten its sense: "Eating lunch, the bottom of my coffee cup sprang a leak." Parallel structures within a sentence or between sentences are useful for making clear either an essential likeness of meaning or a sharp contrast: "From each according to ability, to each according to need."

In addition to making syntactic sense, a writer should strive for a pleasing variety of sentence structures and take into account the subtlest of all the properties of words—their rhythm. Once they are read, even silently, words mark time and take on rhythm. Some writers depend almost as much on rhythmic patterns as on syntax to convey the connections among their words. Repeating and varying the length of phrases or clauses gives memorable rhythm to prose, and memorable rhythm makes memorable prose.

Remember that syntax offers the writer not just a set of rules to be obeyed, but an array of opportunities to be considered. A well-written work acknowledges its occasion and its audience in every way, even in its syntax. On some informal occasions, a writer may properly break what seem to be rules. Experienced writers will work both with and against conventions of syntax just as they work with and against large-scale conventions of organization and evidence. But any such deviations must arise from choice, not ignorance, and through intention, not negligence.

A work of writing is paradoxical. As document, it is always in the past, but as performance, it is always in the present. Its spontaneity is always rehearsed. It is both a means of self-expression and a medium of communication with others. Public and private, the written word not only has meaning, but in some important ways *is* meaning. But perhaps the greatest paradox of all for the writer is that only a concern with these matters, down to the smallest detail, makes writing more than a trifling matter.

4

Verbs: Voice, Tense, and Mood

— ♦ —

Voice

The voice of a verb indicates the relation between a verb and its subject, showing whether the subject undertakes an action (active voice) or undergoes it (passive voice). "I *love* Paris" is active; "Paris *is loved* by me" is passive. For most purposes, write with active verbs. In syntax, as in society, it is better to give than to receive. When you do use the passive, as you occasionally will, make certain that the use is necessary. Although fumbling the tense of a verb may break your reader's attention and puzzle him or her momentarily, the inappropriate use of the passive is likely to have a more lasting effect on the reader: boredom.

Passive verbs can make sentences puffy and evasive. Passive sentences are normally longer than their active counterparts, and the extra words in them are less important and less informative than they seem.

> The plaque *had been placed* on a wall facing the Grand Canal by the Byron Society, which *has been supported* in this act by funds from the British Overseas Council.

> Several of her closest advisers *are reported to have
> been considered* for appointment to the new commis-
> sion.

The first sentence uses the passive verbs to pretend that what it has to say is indeed of monumental importance, whereas the second sentence, more coy or devious, pretends to have more information than it can report. It suggests the possibility of intrigue, or of rivalry, without giving much information. From whom did these reports come? Who actually considered these advisers for the appointment? The passive verbs give the writer a way of not having to say. Not all the vagueness in these sentences comes from the passive verbs, but the use of the passive encourages wordiness and obscurity. Passive verbs often require a dull proliferation of prepositional phrases, like those in the first example.

There are, however, appropriate uses for passive verbs. The passive can, if necessary, shift emphasis from subject to object or from cause to effect:

> This house *was designed* by Frank Lloyd Wright in
> 1922.

If your immediate interest lies not so much with Wright as with the house he designed, the passive is entirely appropriate. You may also use the passive when the exact source or performer of the action is universal, anonymous, impersonal, irrelevant, or unknown:

> Fifty samples *were collected* at half-hour intervals and
> *transferred* to sterile containers for culturing.

> The journal *is published* three times a year, in Janu-
> ary, March, and September.

The passive form is also occasionally useful in breaking a pattern when several sentences in a paragraph begin with the same word or phrase:

> While studying philosophy and medicine at Munich, Brecht sometimes attended a seminar on modern drama at the university. In his spare time, he began to seek out opportunities to hear Wedekind read and perform. *Baal,* Brecht's first play, *was written* at Munich under Wedekind's influence. Brecht composed a number of incidental songs for the play and arranged the scenes after Wedekind's boldly incoherent fashion.

Without the variation from active to passive in the third sentence, the paragraph would read: "Brecht attended, he began, he wrote, he composed." The passive form nicely suggests, in addition, Brecht's receptivity to Wedekind's influence.

Similarly, passive participles can introduce a rhythmic variation to a series of short, clipped sentences or to a string of sentences joined together with *and.*

> She was caught in a familiar dilemma. She didn't know where to turn for help. Her husband would probably think her reckless. Her lover was far away.

> Caught in a familiar dilemma, she didn't know where to turn for help. Her husband would probably think her reckless. Her lover was far away.

Fusing the first and second sentences together by converting the first into a participial phrase makes the parallelism between *her husband* and *her lover* more emphatic. But it *is to be remembered* that the passive voice *must not be used* too frequently in any piece of writing. Most passive verbs, like those in this last sentence, are more annoying than useful.

Tense

Tense is not simply a matter of time. Although the tense of a verb places an action in the past, present, or future, the tense also helps to define other aspects of that action, showing, for example, whether it is habitual or occasional, momentary or ongoing. Although a writer usually chooses the appropriate tense instinctively, the sequence of tenses in a paragraph may present difficulties, and certain tenses have special uses that at first appear to defy common sense.

The Present Tense

Seize the present. Verbs in the present tense can create the illusion that an event is occurring at the moment that it is being described, no matter when the event in fact took place. You should use the present tense, in addition, to summarize the contents of articles and reports or to sketch out the plot of a novel, movie, or play. The performance may be over, but your summary should make it seem to the reader as if the play were being enacted now:

> Misunderstanding her plea, Othello *slaps* Desdemona in the presence of the Venetian ambassadors.

Summarizing a report in the present tense gives it a similar freshness:

> Jensen *recommends* that we move quickly to expand the factory in Lowell. He also *suggests* that we suspend construction on the plant in Framingham.

In contrast, historical facts and descriptions of unrecurring events belong in the past tense:

> Colbert *enriched* the treasury by imposing new taxes and by collecting old ones more efficiently.

Although you should not shift tenses randomly, do not be afraid to shift from present to past or from past to present when the sense demands it:

> Kolb *wrote* the committee report in 1982. The report *begins* with a study of enrollment in the city's
> ✦ schools. It *indicates* that while the number of

elementary-school students has remained constant,
the number of high-school students has dropped by
10 percent.

That Kolb wrote the report in 1982 is stated as historical
fact, in the past tense. The contents of Kolb's report are,
however, summarized in the present tense.

In other circumstances the present tense suggests
continuity and endurance. This use of the present suggests
that the action of the verb is as true now as it was in the past
and will be in the future. Proverbs, rules, and other
categorical statements of fact or belief are expressed in the
present tense:

Loves *conquers* all.

All happy families *are* alike; each unhappy family *is*
unhappy in its own way.

The present tense is also appropriate for expressing normal, habitual, or inevitable actions:

She *practices* law in the city.

The bank *closes* at 3:00 P.M.

The virus *spreads* by contact.

Descriptions and commentaries in the present tense evoke
both immediacy and regularity:

In April, melting snow *forms* pools in ruts and
ditches along the Vermont roads.

The patient *feels* periodic sharp pains in her lower
abdomen.

Even though the physician does not know whether the patient is indeed feeling the pains at the moment the sentence
is being written, the present tense is appropriate here. It
suggests that the attacks are chronic and potentially symp-

tomatic. In this regard, note the contrasting effects of the two verbs in the following sentence:

> I normally *vote* with the director, but today I *voted* against her.

The first verb indicates a habitual action; the second marks an exception. And even though the exceptional vote against the director is more recent than all the other votes, the exception is expressed in the past tense and the habitual action in the present.

The Past Tenses

English provides subtly different ways to describe acts that have already occurred. A writer who discriminates among these ways can convey a precise sense of the duration, frequency, and completeness of the action. Compare the following sentences:

1. Simple Past

> Many lawyers *supported* the Supreme Court's decision.

The verb here describes the support as having begun and ended at a specific or limited time in the past. This sentence could begin: "In 1944," "During the war," or "In the past."

2. Perfect

> Many lawyers *have supported* the Supreme Court's decision.

In this version, the action seems to have begun in the past but to have come to an end only recently. The implication here is that the support has continued over a longer or less definite time than in the first sentence and extended almost to the present moment. "Until now" could be appended either to this sentence or to the first; "until then" or "years ago," only to the first.

3. Past Progressive

Many lawyers *were supporting* the Supreme Court's decision.

In this version, as in the first, the verb describes the support as having begun in the past and having continued for a limited time, such as "during the war." But this sentence implies in addition that the action was continuous throughout that period.

4. Perfect Progressive

Many lawyers *have been supporting* the Supreme Court's decision.

As in the third version, the verb here suggests endurance and continuity, but with the further implication that the action extends into the present. "Until now" could be used with this form of the verb, but not "until then." In contrast to *have supported,* the sense here is that the support is still current, although it may come to an end soon.

Just as the simple past and the perfect tenses refer to a time that is earlier than the present, the past perfect tense is used to mark actions that, from a specific point of reference in the past, seem to have occurred at an even earlier time:

Until the war was over, many lawyers *had supported* the Supreme Court's decision.

Such exactitude is not always necessary, however, and in many cases you may substitute the simple past for the past perfect:

By 1700, American cabinetmakers *began* (instead of *had begun*) to turn away from the designs of their English masters.

Stuffing past perfect verbs into a small space will slow the reader down unnecessarily, as the awkwardness of the following sentence shows: "By 1700, American cabinetmakers *had begun* to turn away from the designs that they *had learned* from their English masters."

Sequence of Tenses

Although few extended pieces of writing lend themselves to simple chronological order, all writing must have a clear and consistent sequence of tenses. Be especially careful about the sequence of tenses within a sentence, for the tense of the verb in the main clause can influence the tenses of the verbs that depend upon it:

> In this morning's paper, the playwright *says* that he *is* tired of the stage and will retire.

> In *The Tempest,* Shakespeare *indicated* that he *was* tired of the stage and would retire.

Remember that sometimes in moving from the main clause to a dependent clause you will have to shift from past tense to present tense in order to indicate that the action of the second verb continues into the present:

> Shakespeare *said* that all the world *is* a stage.

Remember too that present infinitives (to + verb stem) are appropriate after past verbs: Shakespeare intended *to retire* (not *to have retired*) in 1613.

Shifting tenses in a careful sequence allows you to distinguish actions that take place at approximately the same time from those that take place at different times:

> The manager *told* me that she *appointed* a new representative to this district.

> The manager *told* me that she *had appointed* a new representative to this district last month.

In the first sentence, the exact timing of the events is unknown or unimportant. Both the conversation and the appointment are in the past, perhaps roughly at the same time or perhaps not. The second sentence, in contrast, emphasizes the sequence of events: the appointment took place *before* the conversation. Indeed, the sentence might even suggest that the appointment had not worked out and that the representative had since left the firm. When the period of the main verb is specified and the two actions are not simultaneous, the sequential form is preferred.

> The manager *told* me *this morning* that she *had appointed* a new representative to this district.

Participles (verb stem + ending) and infinitives (to + verb stem) are especially useful for distinguishing between actions that occur at the same time and actions that occur in sequence. Use the present participle to express actions contemporaneous with the main verb. Use *having* + past participle to express actions that precede the main verb:

> *Seeking* better wages for his fellow workers, Gompers *undertook* to organize them into a union.

> *Having sought* better wages for his fellow workers, Gompers next *undertook* to improve the conditions in the factories.

Similarly, use the present infinitive to express simultaneity, and the past infinitive to express sequentiality.

> He (now) *seems to be* ambitious (now).

> He (now) *seems to have been* ambitious (at an earlier time).

> He (in the past) *seemed to be* ambitious (at the same time in the past).

> He (in the past) *seemed to have been* ambitious (at an earlier time in the past).

This last form is rarely necessary; the third can often be substituted for it. The exactitude of this double past construction barely compensates for its awkwardness.

Mood

Verbs vary in mood as they do in tense and voice. Verbs in the indicative mood state facts or question them: "She *loves* me." "She *loves* me not?" Verbs in the imperative mood make direct commands: "*Love* me or *leave* me." And verbs in the subjunctive mood express hope, possibility, or obligation: "She insists that he *leave* her alone."

Of these moods, only the subjunctive poses difficulties, and these are easily overcome. Use the subjunctive in hypothetical conditions: "If I *were* king, there would be no taxes." The subjunctive mood here brings out the unreality of the condition. This sense of unreality is lost if you use the indicative: "If I *was* king." Consider the following pairs of sentences:

> If she *drives* through Westport, she will stop by the office. (indicative)
>
> If she *drove* through Westport, she would stop by the office. (subjunctive)
>
> If she *drove* through Westport, she stopped by the office. (indicative)
>
> If she *had driven* through Westport, she would have stopped by the office. (subjunctive)

The indicative forms admit the possibility both of her driving through Westport and of her driving another way. The subjunctive forms, in contrast, suggest that she will probably not drive through Westport or that she has already driven another way. Thus the subjunctive is appropriate to conditions that are doubtful or untrue, and the indicative to conditions that are as likely as not.

Use the subjunctive also in clauses following verbs of exhortation like *move, demand,* and *urge:*

I move that the meeting *adjourn.*

I demand that the chairman *answer* my question.

You may also notice the subjunctive in certain set phrases like "*come* what may" and "far *be* it from me." Many of these phrases are clichés. Avoid them, and avoid other antiquarian revivals of the subjunctive: "If this *be* true, I shall vote against him; it *were* treason to vote otherwise."

CHAPTER

5

Agreement

—— ♦ ——

Agreement Between Subject and Verb

Nouns, verbs, and adjectives may be either singular or plural. The patterns of syntax by which we connect them to one another demand agreement in number. While most writers do not have difficulty with the principle of agreement, everyone encounters occasional problems, especially with compound and collective subjects. Start with the subject. Even when the verb precedes the subject in the sentence, the number of the subject determines the number of the verb:

> After me *comes* the *deluge.*

> There *are* thirteen *ways* of looking at a blackbird.

Phrases and clauses that accumulate between the subject and its verb do not disturb the pattern:

> *She*, as well as several of her cousins, *has traveled* extensively in the Orient.

A *problem* with studies conducted under conditions like these *is* that control groups cannot properly be defined.

Compound subjects (two or more subjects joined by *and*) are almost always plural:

A *congressman* from New York and a *senator* from New Jersey are expected to inspect the construction site sometime this month.

Certain familiar compound phrases may, however, be regarded as singular in form:

Jacket and tie is required after 6 P.M.

Does *bread and butter* really provide important nutrients?

When both parts of a compound subject identify the same person or thing, the verb is singular:

This *outcast and wanderer* turns out to be Wotan in disguise.

When a compound subject follows the verb, especially in a sentence beginning with *there are* or *there were,* you may wish to let the verb agree in number with the nearest noun that completes the sense:

There *was* an oil *painting* and several watercolors in the exhibition.

There *were* several *watercolors* and an oil painting in the exhibition.

There *was* a *Rubens* and a Turner in the exhibition.

These sentences seem acceptable to most readers. The number of the verb agrees with the number of the nearest noun in the compound subject. But strict interpreters of the principle of agreement insist that a compound subject take a plural verb even here:

> There *were* an oil *painting* and several *watercolors* in the exhibition.

> There *were* a *Rubens* and a *Turner* in the exhibition.

You may prefer to rewrite the sentence to avoid the problem:

> The gallery exhibited an oil painting and several watercolors.

Coordinate subjects (two or more subjects joined by *or* or *nor*) require a singular verb when each element of the subject is singular and a plural verb when both elements are plural:

> A *diplomat* or other *official* usually *announces* the decision.

> Neither *banks* nor independent *agencies offer* appropriate life insurance policies.

When one of the elements of a coordinate subject is singular and the other is plural, determining the number of the subject may be awkward:

> Neither *guns* nor *ammunition* $\begin{smallmatrix}\text{is?}\\\text{are?}\end{smallmatrix}$ available to the besieged army.

The neatest solution to this dilemma is to rephrase the sentence so that both elements are the same in number:

> Neither *guns* nor *bullets* are available to the besieged army.

If you cannot recast the sentence, you may allow the verb to agree in number with the element of the subject to which it is closest in position:

> Neither guns nor *ammunition is* available to the besieged army.

> Neither the President nor his *advisers recommend* a change of policy.

> *Does* the *President* or his advisers recommend such a change?

Collective subjects such as *family, group,* and *committee* may be construed as singular or plural, depending on their meaning in context. The paradox of many acting as one creates a moment of grammatical confusion. But number cannot remain equivocal; in each instance, you must decide whether the subject is singular or plural and stick by your decision.

When in doubt, adopt the singular—even for *The United States.* Only if you are considering the collective subject as a number of more or less distinct individuals, not as a unit or aggregate, should the verb be plural:

> The jury *agrees* on the verdict.

> The jury *disagrees* with the judge.

> The jury *disagree* among themselves about the verdict.

In the first and second sentences, the jury seems to act together as a single entity; in the third sentence, the jury no longer acts as a group.

Such fine distinctions are rarely necessary. A singular verb is almost always appropriate to a collective subject.

Expressions of duration used as the subject may be either singular or plural, depending on whether the writer is thinking of the duration as a single period (singular) or as a series of successive units of time (plural):

> Four years *is* the minimum sentence mandated by the new law.

> Five years *separate* Wordsworth's two visits to Tintern Abbey.

Nouns ending in -*s* look plural, but some may in fact be singular:

> *Statistics* is a popular subject.

The tricky noun *number* is usually singular when preceded by the definite article *the* and plural when preceded by the indefinite article *a*:

> *The* number of mistakes *runs* high.

> *A* number of mistakes *are* unavoidable.

The first example refers to a particular, if indefinite, number—the sum of mistakes. The second example refers to several mistakes, committed one after another, so its verb should be plural.

Agreement Between Pronouns and Antecedents

The indefinite pronouns (*any, anyone, anybody, each, everyone, everybody, no one, none, nobody, somebody, someone*) are well named. When any one of them is used, its very lack of definition creates problems of agreement. Indefinite pronouns are traditionally singular in number but deceptively plural in sense. *No one hesitates* to use a singular verb with an indefinite pronoun—as in this sentence—but almost everyone feels perplexed at times when attempting to find the possessive pronouns, *his, her,* and *their,* and the reflexive pronouns, *himself, herself,* and *themselves,* that correspond to indefinite antecedents like *everybody* and *no one.* Everyone must make "his" or "her" or "their" own decision on this complex matter.

The established convention of using *his* and *himself* exclusively is under attack for its subliminal anti-feminism, and yet the more equitable *his or her* and *himself or herself* sound clumsy and legalistic:

> England expects everyone to do *his or her* duty.

There are justifiable objections, nonetheless, to all the usual alternatives. While "England expects everyone to do *his* duty" may suggest, inaccurately, that a woman is free from this responsibility, "England expects everyone to do *their* duty" looks wrong to most readers, although it has become frequent in speech. The eye demands what the distractible ear no longer does, that a word ending in *-one* be followed by a singular pronoun. A common solution to this agreement problem is to recast such sentences into the plural:

> England expects all *citizens* to do *their* duty.

In the plural version, however, the distinct call to individual responsibility has become slurred. A careful writer may retain the liveliness of the original singular construction by deciding to construe the indefinite pronoun as masculine in some instances and as feminine in others. Yet "England expects everyone to do *her* duty" will seem to many readers as polemical and as incomplete as its masculine counterpart. The only sure way out of this dilemma is to work in the plural.

Agreement Between Relative Pronouns and Their Antecedents

The relative pronouns (*who, whose, whom, whoever, whomever, which, that*) agree with their antecedents in number, gender, and person.

> They delivered the package to Harris, *who* was driving down to Santa Cruz in the morning.

Like *Harris, who* is third person singular here so that the verb takes the appropriate form: *was.*

A relative pronoun with compound antecedents is plural; one with coordinate antecedents agrees with the antecedent that is closer to it.

> *You and Luis,* who *are* staying behind, should take all messages.
>
> Is it you or *Luis* who *is* staying behind?

The constructions *one of those who* and *one of those that* simultaneously define a group and distinguish a single member of that group. With these constructions the proper antecedent of *who* or *that* is the plural *those,* not the singular *one.*

> She is *one* of *those who attend* school by day and yet still *hold* down a full-time job.

Remember that although relative pronouns agree with their antecedents in person, number, and gender, they take their case from their use in their own clause.

> Myshkin proposed to offer help to *whoever* needed it.
>
> Myshkin offered help to *whomever* he met.

47

In the first example, the relative pronoun is the subject of the verb *needed*, not the object of the preposition *to*; the entire clause is that object. The correct pronoun is therefore the nominative *whoever*. In the second example, the relative pronoun is the object of the verb *met* so that the correct form is the objective *whomever*.

Note that such parenthetical interruptions as *I believe* or *you see* do not affect the case of the relative pronoun.

> Rousseau replied with an open letter to Voltaire,
> who *he believed* had mistaken the proper role of the
> philosopher.

Although the objective forms of the relative pronouns (*whom, whomever*) seem to be dying out of the spoken language from a lack of exercise, they are often encountered in formal prose. The possessive form *whosever*, though, seems to be faltering even in the written language. There are still suitable uses for *whosever*, although you can almost always rewrite the sentence to avoid using it. Thus, you might write:

> *Whosever* notion it is, it is a bad one.

But better still:

> *No matter whose* notion it is, it is a bad one.

CHAPTER

6

Pronouns
and Nouns

— ♦ —

The Function of Pronouns

Pronouns stand in for nouns. To fulfill this function, pronouns must refer clearly to their antecedent nouns. On occasion the pronoun can anticipate its antecedent, but only when this reversal will not puzzle the reader: "During *his* years in Florida, *Joyner* developed several hybrid strains of caladium." The most frequent problems of ambiguous reference arise when the pronouns *it, this, that,* and *which* are used to refer to an extended statement rather than to a particular noun.

> The strikers were determined to stay out for another month, even if *it* cost them the support of the public.
>
> *Native Son* sold 200,000 copies within three weeks of publication, *which* meant that Wright was suddenly the best-selling modern black author.

Few readers would be puzzled by the first sentence, although the *it* has no proper antecedent. To be strictly correct, you could rewrite the clause to read, "even if *their decision* cost them the support of the public." Many readers would, however, object to the use of *which* in the second sentence. The *which* lacks a proper antecedent (it seems to refer to the whole preceding clause), and the construction drags out the sentence needlessly. Try to find a specific noun to replace *which,* or break the sentence into two:

> *Native Son* sold 200,000 copies within three weeks of publication. Wright was suddenly the best-selling modern black author.

Of all the pronouns, *this* is probably the one most often abused. Avoid using *this* at the beginning of a sentence as a gesture towards summarizing the previous sentence or paragraph.

> The manufacturers of Manchester spoke out in favor of constructing the new canal. *This* was due not only to the more efficient transport of coal and iron ore, but also to the greater access that the canal would bring to distant markets.

This is usually too slight and too vague to bear the burden of being the subject of a long or important sentence. Even *their support* would be clearer and more emphatic than *this.* But the whole phrase *this was due* could be scrapped and *because* substituted in order to join the *not only . . . but also* construction to the previous sentence:

> The manufacturers of Manchester spoke out in favor of constructing the new canal *because* they would profit not only from the more efficient transport of coal and iron ore, but also from the greater access that the canal would bring to distant markets.

At times, the problem is not the absence but the proliferation of antecedents. When a sentence affords more than one plausible antecedent, recast the sentence, making clear to which antecedent the pronoun should apply.

The architects agreed with the subcontractors that it was *their* legal responsibility to insure the unfinished structure.

The reader will normally assume that the pronoun refers to the noun closest to it. If the architects are responsible for the insurance, you should eliminate the pronoun and repeat the noun *architects* in order to make the sentence completely unambiguous:

The architects agreed with the subcontractors that it was *the architects'* responsibility to insure the unfinished structure.

Repetition is better than confusion. Remember that an ambiguous reference can sometimes cause misunderstanding: "Since Jane lied to her mother, *she* should be spanked."

Whenever possible, avoid using parentheses or phrases like *the former* and *the latter* to identify the antecedent:

Melville said to Hawthorne that he (Melville) had written a wicked book.

Melville said to Hawthorne that the former had written a wicked book.

These devices clear up, but do not prevent, the reader's confusion. Simply using a reflexive pronoun or a more exact verb will actually prevent the confusion:

Melville *described himself* to Hawthorne as the author of a wicked book.

Melville *confessed* to Hawthorne that he had written a wicked book.

The Case
of Pronouns

Both nouns and pronouns vary in case according to their use in the sentence, but pronouns show the variation more obviously. Nouns and pronouns in the nominative case (*I, you, he, she, it, we, they*) name the subject of the sentence; those in the possessive case (*my, mine, your, yours, his, her, hers, its, our, ours, their, theirs*) indicate ownership or association; and those in the objective case (*me, you, him, her, it, us, them*) name the object of a verb or a preposition. (For forming the possessive case of nouns, see pages 158–159.)

When complementing forms of the verb *to be* and other verbs that do not take a direct object, nouns and pronouns fall into the nominative case: "If I *were he,* I'd get a second opinion." It is certainly acceptable in a casual letter to indicate your position in a group photograph by writing: "That's *me* in the third row." But the more formal the context, the more strictly you must adhere to the use of the nominative case after forms of the verb *to be:* "It was *she* who filed the protest against the new regulations."

Even when prepositions and conjunctions perform similar functions in the sentence, they have different effects on the case of the pronouns and nouns that follow them. Prepositions are followed by a noun or a pronoun or a phrase including a noun or pronoun: "*until* Thursday; *to* their former home; *by* saving her money." Conjunctions are followed by an entire clause (noun or pronoun + main verb): "*until* the weather improves; *where* they were living at the time; *because* they had saved their money."

The objects of prepositions should always be in the objective case. Do not allow first-person pronouns to drift genteelly into the nominative.

> Between you and *me* (not *I*), this plan isn't going to work.

> This gift is from your uncle and *me* (not *I*).

Pronouns and nouns following conjunctions take their case from their use in their own clause. Several common words—*as, but, before, after, since, until*—are sometimes used as prepositions, sometimes as conjunctions. Be careful to adjust the case of subsequent prepositions accordingly:

Everyone but *him* got a free ticket.

Everyone else got a free ticket, but *he* had to pay.

Than is a conjunction, not a preposition. The nouns and pronouns brought into relation by *than* should be in the same case—nominative, possessive, or objective:

We suffered less than *they*.

Our army suffered fewer casualties than *theirs*.

It hurt *us* less than *them*.

Some common deviations from this pattern cause no confusion, however inelegant they may be: "*She* is taller than *him*." But a lack of coordination can often make a sentence silly. "*Louis* likes good food more than *her*" makes Louis seem more gluttonous than amorous. Here a more complete and coordinate form is needed: "*Louis* likes good food more than *she* does."

The subjects of infinitives (to + verb stem) and gerunds (verb stem + ing) are in the objective case.

His lawyers did not want *him to engage* in a prolonged dispute with the government.

We overheard *him talking* to his lawyers about the hearings.

In formal contexts, when the noun or pronoun serving as the subject of a gerund is put into the possessive case, the writer's emphasis seems to fall on the action expressed by the gerund rather than on the person named by the noun or pronoun:

> I cannot imagine *his* ever accepting their advice.

The difference in emphasis between this possessive form and the objective form in "I cannot imagine *him* ever accepting their advice" is subtle, but—to many readers—real. Whatever division of emphasis is intended, always choose the possessive form for the subject of a gerund at the head of a sentence:

> *His* (not *Him*) agreeing to an out-of-court settlement would make headlines.

Using Pronouns to Refer to the Writer or the Reader

To avoid giving the impression that their methods or results are subjective, scientists and writers in related professions avoid the use of *I*. Impersonal subjects and passive-voice verbs give an appropriate tone of authority:

> The purpose of this research project was to test the current models for describing the development of sea-floor communities.

> Studies of animal-sediment relationships in soft-bottom estuaries have been instrumental to understanding the development of these sea-floor communities.

But whether reporting observations, expressing opinions, or building an argument, most other writers refer to themselves freely and openly as *I*. The usual substitutes for *I* are worse. *This writer* seems clumsy. *Yours truly* is chummy. Passive voice constructions such as *It was assumed by this observer that* or *It was evident that* make non-scientific prose wordy and dull. The real problem with using *I* is not one of immodesty, but one of monotony. A series of sentences all beginning with *I* is offensive, but so would a series of sentences all beginning with *It* or *The Easter bunny.* This problem should be solved not by avoiding *I* altogether, but by varying the structure of your sentences.

We and *one* are sometimes useful in place of *I,* but there are limits to their usefulness. Monarchs style themselves as *we:* "Mr. Disraeli, *we* are not amused." So, too, we are told, do essayists and commentators: "*We* were thinking the other day about the unfavorable balance of payments with Japan." What is appropriate to a queen may, however, seem pretentious in an engineer or economist and silly in a sophomore. *We* is useful for persuading the reader subliminally that reader and writer are engaged in a joint enterprise, but the writer should be sure that the reader is in a position to join in that enterprise: "Watching De Palma's new film, *we* see again and again the influence of Hitchcock's early work." If the reader is unlikely to have seen Hitchcock's early work, and if in fact the observation that the critic makes is a personal one, *I* is the appropriate pronoun to use.

One, the categorical pronoun, is used to express "anyone in that situation."

> At night, *one* should drive slowly through even the
> most familiar intersection.

One has an impersonal sound to it that recommends it to people of reserve. But to many Americans the autobiographical use of *one* sounds false:

> After high school, *one* attended Julliard and played
> in various woodwind ensembles there.

One here is pretentious and class-conscious. It presumes that the reader shares the writer's social station and upbringing:

> *One* always put *one's* teddy bear away on the shelf in
> the morning.

Again, remember that modesty is not a simple matter of pronouns, but the impression that the whole of *one's* style will give. A boast is a boast, whatever pronoun is used.

You is, of course, the correct pronoun for appealing directly to readers, offering them instructions, or giving them information that closely affects them. Be sure that when you use *you,* the pronoun can realistically apply to the audience you're addressing, as it does below:

> Before the new highway was built, it would take *you* over three hours to drive to Dayton.

But consider the following sentence:

> During the Civil War, *you* could be held in prison indefinitely without ever being charged with a crime.

However plausible it is that your readers could have visited Dayton, it is extremely unlikely that they would have been subject to arrest during the Civil War. This so-called "ideal" *you* is a well-established, but often unnecessary or weak construction. Substituting *a citizen* for *you* in the second example would make the point clearer. Sometimes, indeed, use of the ideal *you* can cause an embarrassing confusion between the person addressed and the person being described: "In warm weather, *you* need to shower more often." Similarly, ideal use of *your,* to mean *the average* or *the typical,* should be restricted to casual remarks or jokes: "*Your* full-grown hippo may weigh as much as a pickup truck."

7

The Placement
of Modifiers

Modifiers

A word, a phrase, or a clause that imposes a limit (*modus,* in Latin) upon the meaning of another is called a modifier. In the phrase "the last time that I saw Paris," the words *the* and *last* and the clause *that I saw Paris* all modify *time.* They distinguish the final visit from the first time that I saw Paris and from the good time that I had in Rome. In the adage "Speak softly and carry a big stick; you will go far," the adverbs *softly* and *far* modify the verbs *speak* and *go.* The key to the use of modifiers is to place them as close as possible to the words they modify.

Dangling Participles

Present participles (verb stem + *ing*) can be used as modifiers to emphasize the swift succession of actions or merely to introduce variety into a sequence of similar sentences, such as the following:

> Orwell suddenly felt faint. He collapsed on the stretcher.

Rather than write those two choppy sentences, you could write:

> Feeling suddenly faint, Orwell collapsed on the stretcher.

The participle *feeling,* placed at the head of the revised version above, appropriately modifies the subject, *Orwell.* A participle that does not have a clear association with the noun that it appears to modify is called a dangling participle. Dangling participles are common in speech, where context and intonation usually prevent any misunderstanding. But readers are much less tolerant of dangling participles than listeners might be. Some readers may be serious by nature, but they can laugh themselves silly at inadvertently placed participial phrases such as, "Flying over New York, my head was still spinning with excitement."

Certain present participles, however, have dangled for so long and so often that most readers no longer construe them as the modifiers of the subject. They are treated instead as introductory or transitional devices that modify the sentence as a whole:

> *Considering* the extent of the damage, the cost of the repairs was surprisingly small.

Some past participles may also be used in this way:

> *Granted* that there is room for the ad in your budget, the account executive and I still urge caution.

But even tolerable danglers like *speaking of, barring, owing to,* or *given* can be abused. They may be amusingly askew, even in situations when the intended meaning is clear: "*Speaking of* reptiles, the crocodile at Brookfield Zoo died last week." Famous last words. Whenever you use one of these participial constructions, take notice of the relation of the participle to the subject of the sentence.

Other Dangling Modifiers

Noun phrases and adjectival phrases are also likely to dangle when they are used as modifiers at the beginning of a sentence:

> *An ardent abolitionist in the 1850s,* Grimké's fight for women's suffrage began only after the Civil War.

> *Deeply religious,* the enfranchisement of women seemed to her as imperative as the emanicipation of slaves had been.

The noun phrase beginning *an ardent abolitionist* and the adjectival phrase *deeply religious* are intended to describe *Grimké,* but by their position the phrases look as though they modify the subjects of the sentences, *fight* and *enfranchisement.* Constructions like these seem sloppy, if not really unclear. Both sentences would be improved by rephrasing:

> An ardent abolitionist in the 1850s, Grimké began her fight for women's suffrage only after the Civil War.

> Deeply religious, she felt that the enfranchisement of women was as imperative as the emanicipation of slaves had been.

Many writers try to avoid piling up modifiers at the head of sentences since this construction creates a journalistic or breezy effect. Alternative phrasing may be more appropriate to formal prose:

> Grimké, an ardent abolitionist in the 1850s, began her fight for women's suffrage only after the Civil

War. She had a religious conviction that the enfranchisement of women was as imperative as the
emanicipation of slaves had been.

Impersonal constructions can play host to dangling
modifiers of all kinds:

Reading the report, *it* quickly became apparent that
the entire portfolio had to be reinvested.

Having dismissed the possibility of partial reinvestment, there was no other *option.*

Because the subjects of such sentences are inconspicuous
or delayed, the otherwise necessarily close relation of subject to modifier may be overlooked. No reader would infer
that the report had been read by *it* or that an *option* was
responsible for deciding against partial reinvestment. But
who did read the report and dismiss a partial turnover of
the portfolio? No answer is provided by these dangling
modifiers, and unless the answer can be derived from the
context, the reader may never know.

Misplaced Modifiers

Adverbs like *only, almost, also, even, not,* and *nearly* present
special problems as modifiers, for they can readily slide out
of place in a sentence:

Kilbourn carried *only* one precinct. She lost *even* in
her home district of Douglaston.

The position of these adverbs can easily create an unin-
tended ambiguity: "He *only* drinks tea at breakfast." In
speech the stress placed on *drinks, tea,* and *at breakfast* would
prevent any misunderstanding. The writer, lacking these
resources, must try to find an unambiguous place for the
modifier:

He drinks *only* tea at breakfast.

He drinks tea *only* at breakfast.

Although this strict placement of *only* may appear literary or pretentious, it is still preferable to a casual ambiguity. The strict placement of these adverbs lends precision to a sentence, especially in an important explanation:

Section 9 applies *only* to taxpayers over age 65.

With pairs like *both . . . and, neither . . . nor,* and *not only . . . but also,* the misplacement of the first element of the pair may prove especially confusing: "The plaintiff *neither* contributes money to his son *nor* support." Here the position of the word *neither* creates the expectation that *nor* will introduce another verb:

The plaintiff *neither* contributes money to his son *nor* provides him with support.

If, in contrast, *neither* preceded the noun *money,* it would create the expectation that *nor* will introduce another noun:

The plaintiff contributes *neither* money *nor* support to his son.

Split Infinitives

Although many of the forms of the verb are distinguished by their endings, the infinitive form is marked by the addition of the word *to: to have, to hold, to love, to cherish.* The two words tend to stick close together in the course of a sentence, to resist becoming separated. When modifiers push in between *to* and the verbal part of the infinitive, the infinitive is said to be split. Sometimes the split is awkward. *Not,* for example, would be out of place if it came between

61

to and the verbal part of the infinitive, as in "The board agreed to *not* close the case today." *Not* properly belongs before *to:*

> The board agreed *not* to close the case today.

Parenthetical expressions like *however* and *for example* act like gawky interlopers when they split an infinitive: "The board voted to, *however,* approve the new project." *However* should precede or follow the infinitive. In contrast, adverbs that modify an infinitive sometimes work best when they are placed at the end of the infinitive phrase:

> The board voted to approve the project *conditionally.*

In some long constructions, however, placing the adverb at the end would be awkward, for then too many words come between the adverb and the infinitive it modifies: "The board voted to approve the funding for the improvement of the Camden plant *conditionally.*" Here the adverb *conditionally* seems like a breathless afterthought. It should be moved forward, closer to the infinitive.

In a few instances, splitting the infinitive offers an acceptable way out of unintentional ambiguity. Consider the following sentence:

> The board agreed to *temporarily* halt scheduled improvement of the Camden plant.

If *temporarily* came immediately before *to halt,* the reader would not be sure which was temporary, the halt or the agreement: "The board agreed *temporarily* to halt scheduled improvement of the Camden plant." And if *temporarily* immediately followed the infinitive, the reader would not be sure whether to take *temporarily* with *halt* or with *scheduled:* "The board agreed to halt *temporarily* scheduled improvement of the Camden plant." While it is usually preferable to keep an infinitive intact, the writer who superstitiously shies away from ever splitting infinitives may produce sentences so distorted in shape or in sense that no reader will be able to look at them straight. Infinitives, like logs, must sometimes be split before they can be used.

Necessary and Supplementary Modifiers

Consider the difference between the two passages below:

> Miller has written three books. Her book on the Civil War received bad reviews.
>
> Miller has written one book and two scholarly articles. Her book, on the Civil War, received bad reviews.

In the first example, the phrase *on the Civil War* is needed to identify which of Miller's three books received bad reviews. This passage would make little sense without the necessary information contained in the phrase *on the Civil War:* "Miller has written three books. Her book received bad reviews." In the second example, the phrase *on the Civil War* is not needed to identify the book, since Miller has written only one. The phrase supplies supplementary rather than necessary information, and the two sentences in this example would still make sense if *on the Civil War* were omitted: "Miller has written one book. Her book received bad reviews."

Several different kinds of words, phrases, and clauses appear, according to context, either as necessary or as supplementary constructions. The most common are appositives, participial phrases, and relative clauses.

Appositives

George's wife Natalie was a dancer.

George's first wife, Natalie, was a dancer.

Participial Phrases

The man calling the plays is the referee.

The referee, calling the plays with an expert eye, used his best judgment.

Relative Clauses

I never met a man I didn't like.

Tim, whom I never liked, is moving back into the neighborhood.

Supplementary constructions, whether clauses, phrases, or single words, should be set off from the rest of the sentence by a pair of commas. Necessary constructions are not set off from the rest of the sentence by commas.

That and Which

The presence or absence of that pair of commas is the most obvious sign to the reader of the distinction between supplementary and necessary constructions. But the relative pronouns *that* and *which* may also be used to indicate the distinction. As a relative pronoun, *that* always marks a clause as necessary:

> The report *that* Ms. Fernandes wrote is now regarded as out of date.

When the clause is not set off by commas, the relative pronoun *which* also marks the clause that it introduces as necessary. Indeed most writers use *that* and *which* interchangeably to introduce necessary clauses:

The car *that* caused the accident was driven by an off-duty policeman.

The car *which* caused the accident was driven by an off-duty policeman.

When used with commas, however, *which* is the appropriate pronoun to introduce a supplementary clause:

The accident, *which* was fatal, was caused by an off-duty policeman.

Some writers prefer to use *that* for all necessary clauses and to reserve *which* for supplementary ones only. They are entitled to their preference, but they are merely being superstitious. And they needn't go on *which*-hunts when reading other people's prose. A writer may legitimately use *which* to introduce either a necessary or a supplementary clause, so long as the clause is punctuated appropriately.

The uses of *that* and *which* give rise to other superstitions as well. Partisans of *which* believe that *which* is more literary than *that* is, and they needlessly avoid *that* in formal prose. Still other writers imagine that it is necessary to use *which* to avoid placing a preposition at the end of a clause or sentence:

She wore the dress *that* her mother was married in.

She wore the dress in *which* her mother was married.

Both forms are perfectably acceptable in contemporary prose. You should avoid ending with a preposition only when too many words intervene between the relative pronoun and the preposition, or when too many prepositions pile up: "She was wearing the same dress *that* she went into the restaurant around the corner from the bank *in*." Here the use of *which* would make identification of the dress easier.

In the choice of *which* and *that,* individual preference prevails. But when *that*'s pile up at the beginning of a clause, even the most devoted partisans of *that* must change their habits:

> The only serious objection was *that which* (not *that that*) was raised by the municipal employees.

Yet the phrase *that which* itself is often unnecessary, and you may choose to delete it:

> The only serious objection was raised by the municipal employees.

Or even, simply:

> The municipal employees raised the only serious objection.

Whatever your usual preference, be consistent. Do not switch in the middle of a parallel construction from a *that* to a *which* used without commas.

> *The Faerie Queene* is a poem *that* most teachers love and *that* (not *which*) most students hate.

You may, however, need to use *that* and *which* together in a sentence if *that* has to be used for a necessary clause (without commas) and *which* for a supplementary one (with commas).

> They haven't seen the play *that* Benjamin Glover recommended, *which* is now sold out for its entire run.

That-clauses and *which*-clauses are, of course, subject to the same misplacement as other modifiers. Like other relative pronouns, *that* and *which* refer to the last appropriate noun, which is called their antecedent.

66

> The book reviewed in *Harper's, which* came out only yesterday, was written by the husband of the young professor *that* I introduced to you at my last cocktail party.

Here, *Harper's* seems by its position to be the antecedent of *which,* and *professor,* the antecedent of *that.* It is not clear, therefore, whether it is the book or the magazine that came out only this morning or whether it is the professor or her husband that was encountered at the recent party. An overcrowded party? Or just an overcrowded sentence? Prose needs to be better organized than daily life is, so even if you're the sort of person who can't keep names straight, you should try to keep your modifiers in order and in close conjunction to the words they modify.

Putting Modifiers in Their Places

The placement of modifiers in a sentence determines their relative importance and gives the sentence its own particular slant or emphasis. Even when not misplaced according to the demands of English syntax, a modifier may still be out of place according to the needs of context.

A modifier placed at the beginning or at the end of a sentence normally makes a stronger impression than one placed in the middle. Consider, for example, the differences between the pairs of sentences below:

> Alicia Torres, the Republican senator from New Mexico, won 58 percent of the vote in the 1974 election without campaigning. Her opponent campaigned heavily and lost.

> In 1974, Alicia Torres, the Republican senator from New Mexico, won 58 percent of the vote without campaigning. In 1980, she campaigned heavily and lost.

> In 1974, Alicia Torres, the Republican senator from New Mexico won—without campaigning—58

67

> percent of the vote. In 1980, she campaigned
> heavily and won 43 percent.

The arrangement of words in each of these versions of the sentences about Senator Torres gives an emphasis especially suited to a particular context. The first version stresses her name and the phrase *without campaigning* in order to contrast her victory to the loss of her opponent, who campaigned heavily. The second version draws attention to the year of the election and the phrase *without campaigning* in order to contrast her easy victory in 1974 to her strenuous but unsuccessful campaign in 1980. The third version, interjecting *without campaigning* at an unexpected place in the syntax of the sentence, emphasizes the years, the nature of the two campaigns, and the percentages of the vote.

Play with the order of the elements in a sentence until you find an arrangement that fits. You may be able to improve a sentence for your purposes merely by shifting a few words or phrases. Always be careful, though, not to overload a sentence with modifiers. You risk straining the anatomy of the sentence and may develop a sentence that is top-heavy, flat-footed, or flabby in the middle, like this: "The man's hat, which he had purchased in 1956, when a dollar was worth more than twice what it is worth today, is dark brown."

The problem of finding the best place for the modifiers you need can be tricky. Let your context be your guide.

CHAPTER

8

Repetition
and Variation

— ♦ —

Inadvertent Repetition

Patterns in language, like those in music or architecture, depend upon repetition, but a writer must learn to distinguish an inadvertent repetition from an essential one:

> The union *demanded* that its *demands* for better working conditions be met.

> The union *demanded* unequivocally that its *demands* be met.

In the second sentence, the repetition of *demand* conveys a sense of urgency, whereas in the first sentence, the same repetition seems idle. It is hard to explain just what makes for the difference in effect, but perhaps the reason is that the phrase *for better working conditions* in the first sentence distracts from the repetition and the simpler syntax of the second calls attention to it. Whether you are aiming at emphasis or irony, make sure that when you do repeat a word or phrase, the structure of your sentence is clear enough for the reader to make out your intention.

Some sorts of repetition are so annoying that you should be able to detect them almost as fast as you produce them. The jingle of inadvertently repeated words or sounds is as displeasing to the eye as it is to the ear. The most common sources of such jingling are the suffixes *-ing, -ly, -tion, -ity,* and *-ance,* the conjunction *that,* and the prepositions *of* and *in:* "Kaplan loses cases distressing*ly* frequent*ly.*" Omission or replacement of one of the jingling words will usually solve the problem:

Kaplan loses cases distressingly often.

Parallel Structure

Although inadvertent repetition is easy to expunge, useful repetition is difficult to create and to control. Consider how the parallel patterns of syntax in the preceding sentence emphasize likeness and contrast:

inadvertent	repetition	is easy	to expunge
useful	repetition	is difficult	to create and to control

The parallel syntax of the two clauses makes the contrast in meaning all the more forceful. Usefulness is opposed to inadvertency, difficulty to ease, and creating to expunging. Then the repetition of infinitives at the end of the second clause ("to create and to control") slightly disturbs the parallelism between the clauses to set up a different kind of parallel structure, one that emphasizes a similarity in meaning. This final use of repetition suggests that creation and control are equally difficult—and equally important— to making repetition useful.

The coordinate conjunctions *and, but, or,* and *nor* signal the need for parallel structure in whatever they join:

He is a knave *and*
a fool.

He is a knave *but* not
a fool.

Is he a knave *or*
a fool?

He is not a knave, *nor*
is he a fool.

Failure to maintain parallelism after a coordinate conjunction makes a sentence look sloppy:

He is a knave and foolish.

He is a knave and acts foolishly.

In such sentences the failure is obvious and easily remediable, but with longer sentences the shift from one construction to another may seem more difficult to resist:

The ambassador is *brave, intelligent,* and *shows* great
promise as a negotiator.

Dr. Malone advises her patients *to eat* several small
meals rather than three large ones and *that they
should* abstain from alcohol.

Yet these sentences, too, could be easily straightened into parallel structures:

The ambassador shows *bravery, intelligence,* and
great *promise* as a negotiator.

Dr. Malone advises her patients *to eat* several small
meals rather than three large ones and *to abstain*
from alcohol.

Correlative conjunctions such as *either . . . or, neither
. . . nor, whether . . . or, both . . . and,* and *not only . . . but also*
tend to be especially susceptible to problems of parallelism:
"The committee has suggested *not only* an increase in the
minimum wage, *but also* that the forty-hour week be short-

ened." To rephrase such sentences is no more difficult than to rephrase a sentence like "He is a knave and foolish." Parallel structure requires a correspondence between parts of speech: nouns and nouns, verbs and verbs, adjectives and adjectives:

> The committee has suggested *not only* an *increase* in the minimum wage, *but also* a *shortening* of the forty-hour week.

In order to evoke parallel structure fully, it is necessary to repeat words that might otherwise be omitted from the sentence, particularly the words *a*, *the*, and *that*:

> Ann Lincoln is *the* leader of the district council and (*the*) president of her local school board.

The omission of one of these words looks particularly careless when the word has been left out of a long series of parallel elements:

> Appel interviewed *the* President, Secretary of State, Attorney General, and *the* Secretary of Defense.

Here only the first and the last elements of the series are accorded the article *the* that all elements in a parallel structure seem to require.

Some slippages from parallel structure have become standard, especially in informal prose: "The President asked him *to* come in and sit down." Coming in and sitting down, although not strictly simultaneous, are closely connected parts of a single request, and so it is not appropriate to repeat the *to* that parallelism would normally require: "*to* come in and *to* sit down." But in many sentences, the failure to repeat a key word can lead to an unwanted shift in meaning: "The plaintiffs contend *that* segregated public schools are not "equal" and hence they are deprived of the equal protection of the laws." As it stands, this sentence implies that the schools, not the plaintiffs, are deprived of equal protection. To be clear and accurate, the sentence should properly read:

> The plaintiffs contend *that* segregated public schools are not "equal" and *that* hence they are deprived of the equal protection of the laws.

Syntax, Monotony, and Variation

In writing or rewriting, you should look to see that you have made good use of the choices in sentence structure open to you. You can write in simple sentences, composed of subject, verb, and complement, all in a single clause:

> The rich   have   many consolations.
>
> (subject)   (verb)   (complement)

Or you can join two such clauses together with a coordinate conjunction such as *or, nor, and, but, yet,* or *for,* to place the two clauses on an equal footing:

> The rich get richer *and* the poor get poorer.

Or you can join two clauses with a subordinating conjunction such as *that, which, because, since, while, although,* or *when*:

> People are rich in proportion to the number of things *that* they can afford to leave alone.

Certain occasions, certain formats seem better suited to one sort of sentence than another. Simple sentences seem appropriate to plot summaries and laboratory observations, for instance. But almost any format will admit greater variety in sentence structure than most writers habitually produce. When revising a draft, you should be on guard against overuse of any sort of sentence. A series of simple sentences can make prose appear choppy or dull:

> In Act III, the gypsy women spread out a deck of cards to tell their fortune. The cards tell them of good luck and love. Carmen watches for a while and takes out a deck of her own. She shuffles the cards slowly. Again and again she turns up a spade, the card of death. The gypsy women continue to exclaim over the happiness that is to come to them.

Sentences like these make the reader impatient, and they make the writer seem incapable of making even the smallest intellectual leap.

In contrast, overuse of coordinate conjunctions like *and* and *but* will make your prose limp:

> Lange's division has fallen far behind in production, *but* he has worked at Unitel for thirty-five years, *and* the management is recommending him for early retirement with full benefits.

The coordinate conjunctions here snuff out the logical life of the sentence. Lange's long service is the reason for his being retired rather than merely let go. Some subordination is clearly needed:

> Lange's division has fallen far behind in production, *but because* he has worked at Unitel for thirty-five years, the management is recommending that he be retired with full benefits.

When using subordinate conjunctions, be certain that you know which clause should be subordinated. Compare:

> The play was over, *when* the curtain fell.

> *When* the play was over, the curtain fell.

Sentences need to be shaped. Work with the order of your words until you find a shape that suits the context and best expresses the connections between your ideas.

Inverting the normal order of words, for example, can sharpen the reader's sense of your point:

> Sweet are the uses of adversity.

> Those who have been left out, we will try to bring in. Those who have been left behind, we will help to catch up.

As orators know, repeating words or phrases in reverse order can make a sentence memorable and neat, whether it suggests the proverbial wisdom of the author or promotes a brand of soda pop:

> Machines don't make people; people make machines.

> You like it; it likes you.

Periodic sentences keep the reader hanging. The syntax of these sentences is not complete or clear until they come to an end:

> Having been employed for over forty years, never having taken a day of sick leave, having used only half her vacation time, and having worked hard at her job, she was still awarded no pension.

To be complete, this sentence requires a subject (*she*), a verb (*awarded*), and a complement (*pension*) which is the crucial, and very last, word. Leaving out all the conjunctions and breaking this periodic sentence into several shorter ones would create a sense of deliberate understatement:

> She was employed for over forty years. She never took a day of sick leave. She used only half her va-

cation time. She worked hard at her job. She was
still awarded no pension.

Although less showy than the long periodic sentence, this
rather clipped version has a certain force of its own. Such a
series of parallel sentences can be used to display triumph,
anger, or determination—or any emotion or thought that
develops in marked stages. The use of parallelism is thus
nicely appropriate to polemic or satire, but parallelism also
underlies many of the indispensable techniques of everyday prose, like the sequence of instructions in a recipe or
repair manual.

Expectation and Surprise

Contrast in sentence length and structure can be a powerful stylistic device. A short sentence will provide a neat
pause or summation after a series of long ones:

> Four score and seven years ago, our fathers
> brought forth on this continent a new nation, con-
> ceived in liberty and dedicated to the proposition
> that all men are created equal. Now we are engaged
> in a great civil war, testing whether that nation, or
> any nation so conceived and so dedicated, can long
> endure. We are met on a great battlefield of that
> war.

The first two sentences, which set forth the historical background of the occasion, are long and complex. They are
connected by the parallelism of the phrases beginning with
"conceived" and with "dedicated." The third sentence,
which suddenly brings Lincoln and his audience to the
present moment, is short, simple, and striking.

Effective writing depends as much upon surprise as
upon expectation. You can surprise the reader by deliberately interrupting the syntax of a sentence—you could, for
example, insert a brief "aside" between dashes—or by

blocking the customary flow of one sentence into the next with a bold sentence fragment. Or an exclamation! could be effective. But be cautious. Sentence fragments violently offend most readers, who regard the production of full sentences as the very least a writer can do.

A writer must, of course, build up a pattern of expectation before trying to surprise the reader. Consider how, in this excerpt from a film review, Joan Didion works with and against parallel structure:

> Self-absorption is general, as is self-doubt. In the large coastal cities of the United States this summer many people wanted to be dressed in "real linen," cut by Calvin Klein to wrinkle, which implies real money. In the large coastal cities of the United States this summer many people wanted to be served the perfect vegetable terrine. It was a summer in which only have-nots wanted a cigarette or a vodka-and-tonic or a charcoal broiled steak. It was a summer in which the more hopeful members of the society wanted roller skates, and stood in line to see Woody Allen's *Manhattan,* a picture in which, toward the end, the Woody Allen character makes a list of reasons to stay alive. "Groucho Marx" is one reason, and "Willie Mays" is another. The second movement of Mozart's "Jupiter Symphony." Louis Armstrong's "Potato Head Blues." Flaubert's *A Sentimental Education.* The list is modishly eclectic, a trace wry, definitely OK with real linen, and notable as *raisons d'être* go, in that every experience it evokes is essentially passive. This list of Woody Allen's is the ultimate consumer report, and the extent to which it has been quoted approvingly suggests a new class of people in America, a subworld of people rigid with apprehension that they will die wearing the wrong sneaker, naming the wrong symphony, preferring *Madame Bovary.*

> "Letter from Manhattan," review of Woody Allen's film *Manhattan.* Reprinted by permission of Wallace & Sheil Agency, Inc. Copyright © 1979 by Joan Didion. First published in *The New York Review of Books,* 26:18–19 (August 16, 1979).

Didion uses parallel structure to build up a sense of irony. In the first part of the paragraph, she sets up a series of parallel sentences beginning "In the large coastal cities of the United States this summer" and then neatly adjusts that introductory phrase to "It was a summer in which." Even though the structure of her sentences follows a strict pattern, her tone is casual, and the effect of the tone on the structure is to make the parallelism express summer boredom or idleness. The structure suggests how little variation there is in the attitudes she is describing.

Of course the "list of reasons to stay alive" that Didion cites also shows parallel structure, and Didion's initial use of parallelism takes on the additional implication that Allen's list is no less idle and no more varied than other fashions of the summer. Then Didion closes off her ironic repetition with an ironic surprise. In her final sentence here, the close repetition of present participles (*wearing, naming, preferring*) continues the buildup of parallel structures. But the punch of that sentence depends as much upon what is not repeated (the phrase *the wrong*) as upon what is. The clever modification of parallel structures here distinguishes the flexibility of her writing from the tedium in the lives of those she is writing about. Even if every paragraph cannot—and need not—be as carefully constructed as Didion's is, every writer will occasionally want to be as deliberate as she has been in controlling the repetition and variation of elements in an important paragraph. Sometimes the rhythm of prose is a writer's most effective means of persuasion.

PART III

——— ♦ ———

DICTION
AND
USAGE

CHAPTER

9

The Effect
of Usage on Words

— ♦ —

The Parts of Speech

Syntax describes the relation of words to other words within a sentence; diction, the relation of words to their meanings and of words to the people who use them. These two concerns are closely allied. Conventions of use influence the writer's choice of words and phrases, just as conventions establish the case, tense, or number that the chosen word will take in a particular sentence. Usage—the cumulative record of uses, in which the most recent instances weigh most heavily—determines the limits of what writers can mean by their words.

A long history of use has made certain words syntactically flexible. A single word may live two lives, as a verb and as a noun. Occasionally, the verb takes a different accent from the noun (re-CORD, v.; REC-ord, n.), but in other cases such differentiation by accent is unreliable (re-SEARCH or RE-search, v.; RE-search, n.), and in still other cases nonexistent (re-PLY v.; re-PLY, n.). And some words, like *substitute,* serve readily as verb, noun, and adjective.

Most words, however, have a primary identity as one part of speech and may seem unidiomatic when called upon to play another syntactic role. These days, nouns seem to be hogging all the parts. Nouns have completely upstaged certain adjectives and affected the impression that others make. Readers would be surprised to learn that motorcyclists wear *leathern* (rather than *leather*) jackets and would probably imagine that *woolen* (rather than *wool*) scarves and *golden* (rather than *gold*) chains were made of some blend or alloy.

Instead of seeing nouns modified by adjectives only, most readers have become used to such combinations of noun with noun as "cell biology" and "resource center," and even to such phrases as "college basketball team captain." In time, readers may even come to accept a phrase like "state traffic commission policy study." But naming is not the only way to express meaning, and stringing nouns to nouns stiffens sentences. English syntax offers too many other possibilities for shaping a sentence for a writer to rely exclusively on nouns.

Perhaps even more widespread is the fashion for forming new verbs out of nouns. Each season seems to bring more and more nouns dressed in verb's clothing. The pattern of such transformations is certainly well established. *Mention,* with the *-tion* ending characteristic of nouns, has also been used as a verb since the sixteenth century, and *caution,* since the seventeenth century. To *gift* and to *loan* may seem to many readers recent and corrupt substitutes for to *give* and to *lend,* yet certain uses of the verb *gift* date from the seventeenth century, and *loan* appears as a verb in Webster's Dictionary of 1864. In practice, perhaps a noun is only a word used as a noun, and a verb, only a word used as a verb. But don't force a noun to do the work of a verb merely to avoid a commonplace verb. Most readers will object to a new noun-verb where there is already a clear and eligible verb.

When signs caution motorists to "Drive slow," should they react quick or quickly? Both *slow* and *slowly,* both *quick* and *quickly* have acceptable adverbial uses. Of course not all adverbs end in -*ly*, and idiomatic substitutions have made rare even some that do. *First* usually takes the place of *firstly*, and *fifth* almost always that of *fifthly*. The adverbial counterparts of many adjectives ending in a consonant and -*y* may be so awkward to pronounce that even in writing the tendency is to substitute the adjective: *silly* for *sillily*, *sorry* for *sorrily*, *funny* for *funnily*.

Unlike -*ly*, which seems to show some tendency to drop away, other suffixes attach to words tenaciously. The suffix -*wise*, meaning "in such manner or with regard to," latches on to nouns and adjectives to form new adjectives and adverbs. Undergraduates and bureaucrats have so overworked this suffix that its use now seems almost invariably parodic: "John Hancock was the boldest of the Founding Fathers signaturewise." The suffix -*ize*, which turns nouns and adjectives into verbs, is perhaps the most reviled and yet also the most useful of these suffixes that form new words.

Everyone makes good use of such words as *organize*, *memorize*, *realize*, *emphasize*, and *generalize*. A number of common words were formed by adding -*ize* to proper names, including *pasteurize*, *bowdlerize*, and *galvanize*. Chemists use *oxidize* and *ionize;* doctors, *stabilize* and *catheterize;* psychologists, *socialize* and *traumatize;* librarians, *alphabetize* and *standardize;* musicians, *harmonize* and *concertize*. Some who object to the literary critic's *thematize* will accept the theologian's *anathematize;* some scorn the bureaucrat's *finalize*, but not the jurist's *legalize* and *penalize*. There is nothing intrinsically or semantically wrong with these -*ize* or -*wise* words, or indeed with any word, but readers may nonetheless have their reasons for objecting to the use of them in a particular instance. Some of these reasons will amount to no more than snobbishness, but others have to do with the traditions that bind writers to readers and make them mutually comprehensible. Careful writers must develop both a sense of their audience and an understanding of those traditions.

Changes in the Meanings of Words

The relation between a word and its meaning is, after all, social and historical, not fixed and absolute. Writers today might use a word to express a meaning different from that which their predecessors gave to it, but probably not different from that which their contemporaries and peers understand. There are some clear patterns to the way in which the meanings of words change. Over the years many words lose their positive connotation and become pejorative. *Plastic,* which once described people who showed grace and ease of motion, now refers to things cheaply made and easily broken. *Silly* used to mean deserving of sympathy or compassion. Some words marking the passage of time now mark the time more slowly than they used to. *Presently* once meant "now, at the present moment," but has come to mean "soon"—no doubt in response to a history of false promises. *Soon* itself originally meant "immediately." A few words become more abstract, while others become more literal. *Pollution,* which formerly indicated a moral impurity, now usually refers to a chemical impurity. Words that derive from the names of places extend beyond their point of origin. *Copper* once identified the ore mined on Cyprus, *denim* the cloth woven in Nimes, France, and *bungalow,* the characteristic dwelling of Bengal, India.

Although it is always interesting and often helpful to know the derivation or original meaning of a word, writers who insist on using a word in its earliest sense may display their learning without communicating their meaning. *Depend* comes from the Latin meaning "to hang down." No one today, however, uses it in this sense: The scarf depended from her left shoulder. *Transpire* derives from the Latin "to breathe through," as through the pores of the skin. But now it has the predominant sense of "come to be known" (It transpired at the meeting that the treasurer had falsified his accounts) or even merely "happen" or "occur" (Much transpired at the meeting). And not just meanings of words, but words themselves may become archaic. A contemporary writer would use the conjunction *lest* or the adverb *nay* only in extremely formal prose or in parody.

New Words

While some words fall into disuse and are almost forgotten, new words come into both technical and general use each year. New concepts, new customs, new machines, new fashions—or those that would appear to be new—seem to require either the redefinition of old words or the coining of new words. The widespread use of computers has brought about new meanings for *generate, program, feedback,* and *access* (as a verb), as well as such new compound words as *input, keypunch,* and *printout.* Several of these words have entered everyone's ordinary vocabulary, while others still look and sound technical.

Eponyms are words that derive from the names of heroes, inventors, and other exemplary figures. The botanist William Forsyth gave his name to the *forsythia,* the hypnotist Dr. Franz Anton Mesmer to *mesmerize,* and the instrument maker Adolphe Sax to the *saxophone.* Acronyms are words that are pieced together from parts of other words. *Radar,* for example, is a RAdio Detecting And Ranging system.

Despite the plenty that English offers, writers searching their minds and their dictionaries in vain for the appropriate word may be tempted to get around their frustration by coining a new term or phrase. Given the nature of their work, translators perhaps feel this need more often than other writers and so have been the source of several now common English words. *Individualism* entered the language in 1840, in a translation of Alexis de Tocqueville's *Democracy in America,* and *empathy,* in 1910, as psychologist Edward Bradford Titchener's rendering of *Einfühlung.*

Because other influential writers and speakers adopted these words, *individualism* and *empathy* have come into general use. But many new words—neologisms—never do. The writers who coined them cannot get them into circulation. Indeed, the metaphor implicit in "to coin a phrase" suggests that the value of a new word derives chiefly from its usefulness and credibility as a medium of exchange. Just as only certain members of an economic community have the authority to issue coins, so too a community of writers permits only a few members to devise its new terms. Leading scientists may require new words to explain their data or expound their theories; copywriters may have to come up with new phrases to describe this year's styles or to sustain interest in last year's. But neither the scientists nor the copywriters can be certain that their readers will accept the new words. Perhaps no word may ever be considered counterfeit, but neologists should be careful to restrict newly coined words to circumstances in which they may be honored and, what is more important, used again.

A community of writers and readers defines itself by its familiarity with certain words (or certain uses of words) and even by its disdain for certain other words. These are the written equivalent of the password and the taboo. If this community is regional, its customs of speaking and writing constitute a dialect; if social, slang; if professional, jargon. Those belonging to one of these communities feel, perhaps even need to feel, that they write and speak the same language. Thus although everyone knows what a *pawn* is and what *checkmate* means, only chess players need to understand what a *hippopotamus formation* and an *English opening* mean; most writers and readers have at least a vague notion of what an *electron* is, but only a scientist can comprehend what a *quark* or a *gluon* might be. Such specialized and technical language is too important to be abused by being addressed to an inappropriate lay audience. A bureaucrat's use of such verbs as *prioritize, eyeball, showcase,* and *activate* may make sense and even seem sensible to another bureaucrat, but these words will strike the uninitiated reader as twaddle.

Clichés

If all writing depends on conventions and judgment in following those conventions, some words and phrases depend too directly on the conventions and not enough on judgment. Clichés are formulas so familiar that the reader doesn't have to think in order to understand them. Some clichés are simply old saws like "the exception that proves the rule," or parts of old saws like "the proof of the pudding" (is in the eating). Others are metaphors and imagery that have lost their freshness: "the ship of state, the light at the end of the tunnel, being in the same boat, going back to square one." Some words can become clichés in themselves from being used in the same contexts again and again, like *ambience* (of restaurants), *impact* (of government policies), *relate to* (characters in books or propositions from people), *interact with* (other people), *significant* (anything), *interesting* (everything).

Circumlocutions

Some clichés have at least the merit of compactness. Circumlocutions do not. They are roundabout expressions for what might as readily be said directly. Inexperienced writers mistake circumlocution for an end in itself, or for a means to the end of fine writing. Many long-winded phrases are easy to eliminate: *as to whether* becomes *whether; with reference to* becomes *about; in a manner similar to* becomes *like.* But phrases like these are often embedded in sentences that are evasive throughout and need to be rewritten. "What the speaker didn't know was that the audience was already familiar with Uzo's films" could become simply "The speaker was unaware of the audience's familiarity with Uzo's films."

To dilate is not, of course, necessarily to dilute. Even the Gettysburg Address, a model of tight prose, begins with a roundabout way of expressing *eighty-seven years ago.* Writers sometimes need such effects in contrast to their

87

plain style. Expressions involving the fewest and shortest words are not always the most exact. Sometimes the topic demands hard words and complicated syntax, and the occasion for writing may dispose the writer to break through the ordinary barriers of expression.

Euphemisms

Euphemisms are a special type of circumlocution, and they too have their appropriate and inappropriate occasions. Older euphemisms like *house of ill repute* and *gone to their reward* evade potentially embarrassing matters of sex and mortality. Many of these euphemisms have outlived the prohibitions that gave rise to them and are now invoked only in parody, like *in a family way* or *comfort station*. But others have become so habitual that writers may inadvertently apply them to ludicrous effect: "The block association asks residents not to let their dogs *go to the bathroom* on the newly seeded lawn."

Many newer euphemisms maintain the tradition of evasiveness. Embezzlers have become *white-collar criminals,* and some houses of prostitution advertize themselves as *massage parlors*. But other new euphemisms seem devised not so much to lessen embarrassment as to enhance prestige. Razors are now sold as *shaving systems,* legal researchers are upgraded to *paralegals,* and raw carrots and celery are *crudités*. Some euphemisms may serve an important social purpose. The general adoption of the term *Down's syndrome* may make possible a more sympathetic and scientific attitude towards the child who has certain congenital anomalies. The term *senior citizen* may or may not bring about greater respect for older men and women. In general, however, as the cliché goes, "say what you mean."

Yet except for some legal constraints, writers are not always obliged to mean what they say. Sincerity is not the ultimate goal of writing. Indeed, one of the great pleasures of writing comes from feeling both an identification with your words and an independence from them. Developing a style, and thinking of that style as only one of many possible ways of expression, frees you from being locked into saying the same things over and over in the same words. You will truly care about your words only when you care for them because they are yours and because they are not you.

CHAPTER

10

Alphabetical Glossary of Words and Phrases

— ♦ —

Writers need to mind their **a**'s more than they do their *p*'s and *q*'s. The indefinite article *a(n)* often slips into sentences where it is not needed. This superfluous *a* is most often triggered by expressions like *kind of, sort of, type of, no less, no better*: "What kind of (a) fool do you think I am?" "Can you find no kinder (a) term to describe me?" But leaving an *a* out of a compound construction may create a misunderstanding. Consider the difference between "I met an artist and a writer at the party" and "I met an artist and writer at the party." Were two people met, or only one? In abbreviated forms of writing like laboratory reports, leaving out an *a* may be a useful shortcut: "(An) examination of the culture revealed the presence of coliform bacilli." Using this shortcut in a more spacious context, such as a book review may make the review sound like a lab report: "(A) quick examination of the table of contents reveals startling omissions."

About is unnecessary when another word or phrase suggests approximation: "They estimate I have (about) a 50 percent chance of recovery."

Like the Latin *infra* and *supra,* the words **above** and **below** may be used to describe the relative placement of items in a text. *Above* describes a passage before the passage now being read; *below* describes one after it: "The article *above* discusses the possible redundancy of *about.*" If you find this phrasing fussy, you may find that you can omit the words without a loss of clarity: "These *statistics,*" for example, instead of "The *statistics* cited above." Using *above* and *below* as nouns (the *above*) or as adjectives placed before nouns (the *above* statement) may give your prose the tone of a subpoena. Placing *above* and *below* after the noun will be less legalistic: "the statement *below,*" "the passage *above.*" Whenever you use *above* and *below,* bear in mind the limits of your reader's memory and patience, and provide page numbers for distant references, such as: "the statement cited *above,* page 23."

By, rather than *to* is the preposition that goes best with **accept:** "Lopez was *accepted* by the Yale Law School." **Admit,** however, takes *to:* "Lopez was *admitted* to the Yale Law School."

Acceptable has become a bureaucratic euphemism with fatalistic overtones. It seems to mean *barely acceptable* or *acceptable, but undesirable.* "The air quality today is *acceptable,*" the Weather Bureau reports, and the Justice Department finds that "the level of crime in our cities is *acceptable.*" Such a use of the word is, in its own terms, *acceptable.*

Be careful about using **according to** as a form of attribution. Unless the context suggests otherwise, as in "*according to* the Bible," "*according to* Hoyle," *according to* may imply that the speaker is not to be believed: "*According to* the defendant there was no possible motive for the murder."

Use **actual** and **actually** to draw a distinction between possibility and fact: "The potential uses of solar energy are boundless, but its *actual* applications are limited by the state of solar technology." If you use *actual* and *actually* merely to add emphasis, you risk sounding casual or incredulous: "The chairman of the board *actually* announced an increase in dividends." At the end of the sentence, *actually* is deadwood: "The news made us happy (, *actually*)."

Before using the phrase **add an additional,** check your arithmetic. You're adding twice.

In a sentence like "My broker *advised* me to sell my shares," **advise** means *give advice.* This sense is lost when *advise* is used merely as an elegant variation for *say* or *tell:* "My broker *advised* me that shares in Telco were now available." Here the broker is offering information, not advice.

The similar pronunciation of **affect** and **effect** often causes them to be confused. The verb *to effect* means *to bring about, to make happen:* "The negotiators *effected* a compromise." The noun *effect* means *result, issue, consequence:* "The *effect* of the compromise was negligible." *Effects,* the plural, describes items of personal property. In contrast, *affect,* which is usually a verb, means *to display, to imitate, to put on, to pretend to:* Ben Jonson said that Spenser *affected* the language of the ancients. But *to affect* can also mean *to influence, to have an effect* (with an *e*) *on:* "Jonson's criticisms did not *affect* the popularity of Spenser's poetry." Psychologists, and only psychologists, use *affect* as a noun meaning *emotion* or *emotional behavior:* "She watched the accident without obvious *affect.*"

Perhaps because the *d* in **aged** is pronounced faintly in phrases like "aged twenty-one," it is sometimes carelessly dropped in writing: "A man, age twenty-one." The whole word can often be dropped without any loss of meaning, or the phrasing can be changed: "A twenty-one-year-old man."

93

The colloquial **all right** is sometimes spelled *alright* in order to indicate its colloquialism. But if you want to use this expression in a formal piece of prose—you may well prefer not to—spell it as two words.

Along with can sometimes cause problems in agreement by making you think there is a compound subject. "Pritchard, *along with* Spitzer, supports her candidacy." Make the verb singular to agree with the subject, Pritchard. See Agreement, Chapter 5.

Also is an adverb, not a conjunction. Used by itself, it cannot link one noun or sentence to another: "The doctor prescribed aspirin, *also* rest." "I went to the barber, *also* I went shopping." In both these sentences a conjunction is needed: "The doctor prescribed aspirin *and also* rest." "I went to the barber *and* I *also* went shopping." The adverb *also* is often redundant when used with *the same,* or *a similar:* "Holmes was trying a difficult murder case. Brandeis was (also) trying *a similar* case."

For the distinction between **among** and **between,** see **between.**

Amount is used to describe a quantity of something that cannot be counted or enumerated: "a small *amount* of butter," "no *amount* of courage." If you can count the items in the quantity, use *number* instead of *amount:* "a *number* of women," "a *number* of houses." Thus you have "a large *amount* of cash" if you carry "a great *number* of dollar bills" in your wallet.

The Greek roots of **analysis** and **analyze** provide good hints on how to use the words. The roots are *ana (apart)* and *lyein (to loosen, to break). To analyze* is to break something or idea into its parts and examine their relation. When a chemist *analyzes* a substance he breaks it into its constituent elements. A psychoanalyst attempts to do the same with the human personality. An *analysis* is not just a thought or an opinion, as one might think from such casual phrases as "in my *analysis*" or "in the final *analysis*." An *analysis* is a systematic scrutiny of parts that make up a whole, and *to analyze* requires one's fullest attention.

Do not be afraid to begin a sentence with **and** or **but**: "*And* God said, Let there be light, and there was light." The placement of *and* or *but* at the beginning is a matter of punctuation and of emphasis, not of syntax. Consider the differences in emphasis created by the way *and* and *but* are used in the three passages below:

> The district attorney asked for a retrial, *but* the judge refused, *and* the defendant was freed.
> The district attorney asked for a retrial. *But* the judge refused, *and* the defendant was freed.
> The district attorney asked for a retrial, *but* the judge refused. *And* the defendant was freed.

The first passage stresses the sequence of events; the second calls attention to the judge's refusal; the third emphasizes the outcome. Sometimes the length and rhythm of a sentence will influence your choice. You might choose, for example, to close off a long sentence with a period and begin the next with *And,* rather than to join the two with a comma.

And/or proves useful in legal or official documents but stands out as jargon in other contexts.

To make your state of mind clear to others, preserve the distinction between **anxious** (*worried*) and **eager** (*looking forward with pleasure*). Thus you may be *anxious* to see the plane land and *eager* to see your friend step off it.

See pages 45–46 for problems with **anybody, anyone.**

As you read this entry, consider the difference between *as* and *because*. In the previous sentence *as* has a clearly temporal sense: *at the time you read.* The prevalence of this temporal sense is a good reason to avoid using *as* in place of *because.* If you do, you risk confusion: "*As* I blew my whistle, Rover ran towards me."

The phrase **as follows,** often used to introduce a list, is an impersonal construction, an ellipsis for "*as* (it) *follows.*" Thus *follows* does not have to agree with the plural number of items that may in fact follow: "The names of those absent without leave read *as follows:* Custer, Mitchell, Patton, MacArthur."

The adverb **back** is redundant with many verbs that themselves connote *back,* especially verbs with the prefix *re-:* "Jones returned the order (back) to the wholesaler."

Background is such a popular word that it comes readily to hand, even though a more precise word may wait in the memory: "Sally comes from a poor *background* (family);" "Suntex is looking for someone with an engineering *background* (an engineer)"; "Her *background* in Middle Eastern affairs (work in the Middle East) makes her a good candidate for the ambassadorship." *Background* is useful in suggesting not merely a single fact or a single kind of supplementary information, but the whole range of circumstances behind a person or event: "A century of colonial rule provides the *background* for the current politics of the Palestinian Arabs."

A **base** or **basis** is a foundation that supports all that rests on top of it. Einstein's theory of relativity, is, for example, "the *basis* of much twentieth century physics." The verb *base* describes the same relation between structure and foundation: "Much twentieth-century physics is *based* on Einstein's theory of relativity." But the phrases *on the basis of* and *based on* are often abused. They appear as casual substitutes for *because of, for the sake of, for,* and *by:* "I chose Miller for the position on the basis of (because of) his excellent record as a salesman." "The rank-and-file adopted the resolution on the basis of (by) a show of hands." Using *based on* in this way is similarly imprecise, and it may lead to a grammatical problem as well: "*Based on* the results of the Gallup poll, Harrison has little chance of winning the primary." Here some readers would consider *based on* to be a dangling modifier; see page 58.

Correct the redundant *the reason is* **because** to *the reason is that. Because of* after a negative clause may create an ambiguity: "The book is not popular *because of* its style." Is the book unpopular because of its style? Or is the book popular, not because of its style, but because of its contents?

Being sometimes introduces a dangling modifier: "*Being* tired, the ballet put me to sleep." See Modifiers, Chapter 7.

Use **beside** for *next to*, as "to stand *beside* her," and **besides** for *in addition to* or *other than*, as "to rely on no one *besides* her."

The difference between **between** and *among* depends not on the number of objects or people being related to one another, but on the nature of that relation. *Between* defines with as much precision as circumstances allow the relation or relative position of a person or thing to each of the other people or things being considered: "Illinois lies *between* Indiana, Wisconsin, Iowa, Missouri, and Kentucky." *Among* expresses a vaguer relation: "Illinois is *among* the most populous states in the nation." As a preposition, *between* always takes the objective case. "Between he and I" may seem correct socially, but it is incorrect grammatically. The correct form is: "between him and me." See The Case of Pronouns, page 52.

Biannual means *twice a year*, but **biennial** means *once in two years* or *lasting for two years*. **Bimonthly** means *once in two months*, and **biweekly**, *once in two weeks* or (more loosely) *twice a month.* Most readers find all of these words confusing or distracting. To avoid this confusion, write out the time scheme in full. Use, for example, "twice a year" instead of *biannual,* or "once every two years" instead of *biennially.*

The cliché **blank check** and its French counterpart *carte blanche* have been overdrawn. Cancel them out of your prose.

Since **both** indicates the likeness of two people or things, its use with another word suggesting likeness is redundant: "*both* men looked alike"; "*both* men are equally handsome"; "*both* men have the same handsome face"; "*both* men looked handsome together." For the same reason, *both* is redundant if used with *as well as,* rather than with *and:* "Both Johnson as well as Kennedy were Democrats." Be careful to avoid misplacing *both . . . and.* "Nixon voted *both* against Kennedy and Johnson" should be rewritten: "Nixon voted against *both* Kennedy and Johnson." See pages 71–72.

A **breakthrough,** in the sense of scientific discovery, is by definition both *new* and *major* so that the word does not need to be qualified by either of these adjectives. If you are tired of reading about *breakthroughs,* try using another word: *discovery, achievement, invention, accomplishment.*

The conjunction **but** may be used to begin a sentence; see *and,* page 95. But be careful not to use two *buts* in succession: "Everyone has heard of hemlock. *But* most people think that the poison hemlock comes from the hemlock tree. *But* in fact it is derived from the fruit of the herb hemlock, a member of the carrot family." The second *but* can be deleted altogether.

Many of the prepositional phrases formed with **case** are indispensable: "In *case* of fire, break glass;" "in no *case* leave the room"; "I shall wire the payment in any *case.*" These phrases avert such cumbersome circumlocutions as "If fire should break out." But the similar prepositional phrase *in the case of* is often merely a makeshift way of making a transition or getting a recalcitrant sentence started: "In the *case* of Shakespeare, thirty-six of his plays survive." Simply rewrite: "Thirty-six of Shakespeare's plays survive."

Cease and **commence** survive in a few formal locutions: *cease* and *commence firing, cease and desist, cease work.* Using them instead of *stop* or *start* lends a strong formal note: "We may look forward to the day when the sound of the cannon will *cease* to be heard and the flight of the dove will *commence.*" This formality may be just what the speech-writer seeks, but in more workaday writing, *cease* or *commence* will seem absurdly ornamental: "The bus *ceased* moving."

The geometry of the expression **center around** disturbs some, who prefer *center on,* or *center in:* "His book *centers on* the first year of Roosevelt's administration." "Political authority centered in the king." *Center on* and *center in* emphasize the main subject of the book and the concentration of authority in the king. But writers are sometimes misled into using *around* when they really wish to stress not the center but the circumference: "His entire political philosophy *centers around* the rights of the individual." Perhaps *revolves around* would be more appropriate, for it at least has the advantage of not offending those with a strict sense of verbal geometry.

Channel, as both a noun and a verb, is now in fashion as a metaphor for *pass, direct, direction.* "Washington is so crisscrossed with *channels* of influence, that lobbyists must *channel* their programs towards the right objective.

Like *in the case of* and *the nature of,* the phrase: *of a* _____ **character** sometimes provides the cover for a circumlocution: "The engineering department recommended a program *of a more efficient character.*" Here the phrasing detracts from the force of the adjective, which would stand out more clearly on its own: "a more efficient program." Sometimes *the* _____ *character* is used to fill the place of an abstract noun. In the following sentence, for example, *efficiency* is the word wanting: "The engineers criticized *the inefficient character* (the efficiency) of the plant."

Writers resort to **clearly** as if to a magic formula, in the hope that the mere invocation of the word will clarify their muddy rhetoric: "Localized areas of the library are *clearly* expected to be subject to periodic interruptions of electrical service." Sentences like this need rewriting, not the addition of *clearly:* "Some parts of the library will occasionally be without electricity."

Most writers still observe the traditional distinction between **compare to,** meaning *to liken,* and **compare with,** meaning *to point out similarities and differences.* You could compare the sound of waves *to* the noise of a crowd, but you would compare the waves on the Jersey shore *with* those on Malibu.

Complex sometimes adds nothing to a sentence, especially to an excuse: "Because of the *complex* legal problems posed by her arrest, Senator Fields does not wish to make a statement."

Even the most cautious writer may stumble over **compose** and **comprise,** words whose similar sound obscures their different applications. *Compose* describes putting parts together into a whole: "Mahler *composed* his Third Symphony in 1896." *Compose* is frequently used in the passive: "The symphony is *composed* of six movements." *Comprise* describes how the whole includes the parts. It is thus similar in meaning to *is composed of:* "The symphony *comprises* six movements." To make matters even more confusing, *com-*

prise is also sometimes used in the passive, to call attention to how a variety of parts are concentrated in a whole: "Many different rhythms and harmonies are *comprised* in the first movement."

A **concerted** *effort* is a phrase frozen in continued usage. You may be surprised to learn that the primary definition of *concerted* is *mutually contrived or agreed upon, done in concert.* Thus *a concerted effort* should be not a merely strong effort, but one undertaken by many.

On the **condition** *that* should never be used merely as a synonym for *if.* It calls special attention to the singular importance of the condition, and it is often used to identify the grounds of a concession: "You will be forgiven *on the condition that* you repent."

When the hammer of a gun *contacts* the firing pin, the gun fires. Here **contact** is close to its most concrete meaning: *to touch.* Today it is most often used figuratively as a blanket term for the many ways one person *gets in touch* with another: *meeting, letter, telephone.* If you are unsure about the form of communication, *contact* can be just the right word. But don't neglect other verbs that describe the exchange more specifically: *ask, call, consult, confer, write to, telephone, see.*

Continuous and **continuously** are applied to actions that continue without interruption: the movement of the earth around the sun, the circulation of the blood, the cycle of the seasons. **Continual** and **continually** are applied to actions that are repeated at intervals. You may complain, for example, that "it rains *continually* in London," or that "the *continual* interruption of the telephone" has broken your concentration.

During the **course** *of* is excessive. *During* will serve by itself.

When a bank **credits** your account, you get more money. The bank adjusts the balance in your favor. Similarly, you *credit* someone for something when you believe in him or bestow favorable recognition on him. You may *credit* your mother for teaching you to balance your checkbook carefully. But in the passive, *credit* is sometimes used sloppily, in reference to unfavorable actions: "The terrorists *credited* with the July 4 bombing have escaped." If the verb were active, the illogicality of *credit* would be apparent: "I *credit* the terrorists with the July 4 bombing." In such contexts, try *hold responsible for* or *accuse of.*

Crisis *situation* is redundant. In formal prose, *crisis* must give a sense of *a turning point* or *a decisive moment.* In casual use, *crisis* simply becomes *a continuing state of danger or disarray:* "In the tenth day of the strike, the garbage *crisis* seems to be worse in the suburbs than in the city."

The English noun **data,** meaning *set of facts, information,* is taken from a Latin plural noun meaning *things given.* If its sense in English is collective, it receives a singular verb: "The *data* reveals a startling discrepancy in the budget." If you wish to stress the individuality of each piece of information, you may use a plural verb: "The *data* are to be collated in three categories." See collective nouns, page 44.

The prefix **de-** gives you the freedom to use or even to create a special verb to describe the elimination of nearly anything. You can *defrost* a refrigerator, *defog* your rear windows, *debug* your office, or *debrief* your colleagues so that they will not reveal what you had once briefed them about. You may wish to exercise this freedom in order to simplify a long technical explanation (*defluoridate*) or to create a fanciful word like *de-Shakespeare.* But remember that the new word may well appear silly or tedious to your readers: "This article urges you to *de*prefix." And you will be wise to desist from some new promotional terms formed on analogy to *debark* and *depart:* Airline officials now tell you to *deplane,* and railroad conductors to *detrain.*

The enduring colloquialism *a great* **deal** will look folksy in formal writing: "The new budget will save the company *a great deal* of money."

Definite and **definitely** are often used unnecessarily in the vain attempt to stiffen a phrase that a writer feels is too weak to stand on its own: "Cigarette smoking is *definitely* bad for the lungs." Use these words only when definition—not emphasis—is required: "My client will not sign the contract until the terms for the dissolution of the partnership are stated *definitely.*" "The *definite* structure of her essay makes it easy to read."

Despite the precision promised by the quantitative term **degree,** phrases like *to a great degree* and *to a serious degree* do not make a statement more precise than either *greatly* or *seriously* does.

Don't drop *upon* or *on* from the phrases **depend on** *whether* and **depend upon** *whether.*

Develop, from a French word meaning *to unwrap,* should be used to describe a setting forth by degrees or in detail. A debater *develops* an argument step by step. A composer *develops* a theme by working out changes in the rhythm and harmony. A photographer *develops* film by bathing it in chemicals that gradually bring out the image. Similarly one *develops* something by promoting its growth or expansion gradually. A weightlifter *develops* strong shoulder muscles. A beer drinker may over the years *develop* a pot belly. Anything one *develops* may in turn be said *to develop:* "A child's ability to walk *develops* during his or her first year." *Develop,* then, should not be made synonymous with *happen,* as it has been, for example, in the following sentence: "A revolution *developed* this morning, when leftist guerillas seized the Presidential Palace." And *development* is not a synonym for event: "Recent *developments* in Poland indicate a sharp turn to the right."

Different poses a notorious problem in usage: *different from* or *different than.* When *different* introduces a contrast between one noun and another, *from* is clearly the best choice: "Apples are *different from* oranges." But if a whole clause is to follow *different,* the use of *from* may demand some clumsy sidestepping, since the preposition *from* must have a noun as its object: "Burgundy goes well with *different* dishes *from* those that go well with Muscadet." In such circumstances, you may choose to avert the circumlocution by using *than* instead of *from:* "Burgundy goes well with *different* dishes *than* Muscadet does."

Since **discuss,** as a transitive verb, demands an object, clauses such as *as we discussed* or *as was discussed* sound awkward: *"As was discussed* last night, the transit proposal will increase the budget by five million."

Disinterested means *impartial.* Use *uninterested* to mean *not interested in* or *bored by.*

Whether or not **due to** is an acceptable dangling modifier is still being debated by experts. Many insist that *due to* can be allowed to dangle without harm: *"Due to* the weather, school is cancelled." Of course, school is not due to the weather—the cancellation is. Many similar danglers, like *considering,* or *given,* are unobjectionable (see Modifiers, Chapter 7). Objections to *due to* may linger because it is so easy to avoid the issue altogether by writing *because of.*

Although **each other** and **one another** resemble the pronouns *everyone* and *everybody,* they behave differently. *Each other* is equivalent to *each . . . the other; one another* to *one . . . the other.* "We dislike each other" is an elliptical way of saying "We each dislike the other." Because these constructions each thus comprise two words, they cannot serve as the subject of a verb, for one noun or the other would have to be the subject: "We dislike what one another writes." Changing the number of the verb to plural won't help: "We dislike what one another write." You must rewrite: "We each dislike what the other writes."

On **each** as a pronoun, see Agreement, Chapter 5.

For the difference between **effect** and **affect,** see **affect,** page 93.

Effective as an adverb meaning *after, on, beginning* or *from* is bureaucratic: "The tax rate will be raised 5 percent effective January 1, 1984."

The abbreviation **e.g.,** a vestige of the medieval manuscript tradition, stands for *exempli gratia,* meaning *for example.* **I.e.,** another scribal form, stands for *id est,* meaning *that is,* and is used to introduce not an example but an equivalent, *i.e.,* another way of saying the same thing. Both abbreviations are appropriate only where extreme conciseness is demanded (*e.g.,* definitions, footnotes, charts). Otherwise use *for example* or *for instance* for *e.g.* and *that is* or *namely* for *i.e.*

Either means one or the other of two: "I will not marry *either* of the twins." Used in reference to one of a group of more than two *either* suggests bad arithmetic: "I will not marry *either* of the triplets." On *either* and problems with number, see Agreement, Chapter 5. On the placement of *either,* see Modifiers, Chapter 7.

To **eliminate** something is to get rid of it, to throw it out the door—*eliminate* comes from the Latin *ex* (*out*) and *limen* (*threshold*). In order to be thrown out, something must first have been present. What may happen in the future can be prevented or averted, not *eliminated:* "The negotiators hope that the new terms of the contract will prevent (not *eliminate*) a possible strike by Local 105."

Eminent means outstanding: "Many think the ambassador an *eminent* statesman." **Imminent** means ready to take place, threatening: "The attack is *imminent.*"

Don't use **employ** as an elegant substitute for *use.* One *uses* a screwdriver to turn a screw, one does not *employ* it. Reserve *employ* for special kinds of use, such as using the services of a person ("The firm *employs* more than thirty people") or using something advantageously ("Jones *employed* his time well").

Products and results are by definition what one ends up with, so that the phrases **end product** and **end result** are usually redundant. Use them only if you wish to draw a distinction between an *end product* and a *byproduct.*

The adjective **enormous** means *uncommonly large,* but the noun **enormity** connotes *monstrous wickedness, offense that departs outrageously from the moral norms:* "We must never forget the *enormities* of Auschwitz."

Equally as is redundant: "Peter is *equally as* good as Paul." Use one or the other: "Peter and Paul are *equally* good" or "Peter is *as* good as Paul."

Either something is **essential** or it is not. Comparisons like *more essential(ly)* and *less essential(ly)* diminish the essential force of the word.

Like *e.g.* and *i.e.,* **etc.** belongs only where space is short: technical reports, definitions, footnotes, etc. Although *etc.* stands for *et cetera,* meaning *and other things,* it is commonly applied to people as well. **Et al.**—*et alii, and other people*—is found in bibliographical references to works with several authors.

For problems of agreement with **everybody** and **everyone,** see pages 45–46.

The cumbersome phrase **extent to which** usually means no more than *how much, how far,* or *how strongly,* any of which should be used instead: "Horatio did not know the *extent to which* Hamlet was mad (how mad Hamlet was)." *Extent* is appropriate, however, if used in reference to space: "Dr. Horatio did not know the *extent to which* the disease has spread."

Facilities is a euphemism for *toilet* (itself a euphemism), and **facility** often leads to circumlocution: *medical facility* for a *hospital, educational facility* for a *school.*

The fact that is usually superfluous and can be cut down to *that:* "McKinley admitted (*the fact*) *that* the exhibition was boring." *The fact that* is most objectionable when applied to what is not fact but opinion or speculation: "McKinley admitted *the fact that* the exhibition might not open on time." Sometimes writers superstitiously use *the fact that* at the beginning of a sentence to seem authoritative: "The fact that the exhibition was a bore did not deter McKinley from urging the public to attend." Rephrase the sentence rather than resort to *the fact that:* "Although the exhibition was boring, McKinley did not hesitate to urge the public to attend."

Factor is one of the most common filler words. It saves a lazy writer from finding a better turn of phrase: "The high price of gasoline is an important *factor* in declining (has contributed to the decline in) automobile sales." "In designing a house architects must consider the human *factor* (human needs, the person who will live there)."

Feature, like *factor,* is often merely verbal putty: "A *feature* of Pope's poetry that Byron imitated was the ironic antithesis." Use *feature* to describe a physical form: "Van Gogh

107

was moved by the bright *features* of the Provencal landscape."

Writers of scientific articles and police reports sometimes use **female** *and* **male** as nouns: "The subject, a *male*, showed symptoms of liver failure." "Officers arrested a white *female*." Here the clinical or official impersonality of these words is perhaps appropriate, but don't let *female* and *male* become casual synonyms of *woman* and *man*. Animals, plants, and plumbing fixtures may be *female* or *male*, but only a human being can be a woman or a man.

Few and **fewer** are applied to plural nouns: "*few* people, books, countries." **Less** is applied to singular nouns that indicate an amount: "*less* milk, courage, time." But *less* can also be applied to plural nouns that represent an amount of time, money, or distance: "*less* than 5 minutes, 600 miles, $40."

Finalize is still to be found only in bureaucratic and commercial prose, where it means put in final form: "Our contract with Crumbex has not been finalized yet." Why not *finish, complete, settle, sign, approve?*

For the purpose of is usually unneeded: "The firemen brought a hose *for the purpose of* dousing (to douse) the fire." **For the reason that** often means no more than *because.*

Fortuitous means *accidental,* or *by chance:* "My *fortuitous* meeting with Brickley last week brought to mind our days in London." **Fortunate** means *lucky:* "My *fortunate* meeting with Brickley last week made me a hundred dollars richer."

The Gaelic expression *go leor,* meaning *enough,* has produced the English adjective **galore.** Today the word seems old fashioned and fancy, like the hawker who promises *bargains galore.*

The manager who uses **game plan** to describe a strategy in business or politics is using a flabby, second-string phrase.

Use **garb** for clothing only if you wish to sound quaint or wry: "Designer jeans are standard *garb* in the 1980s."

Clichés like **a garden variety** should be weeded out of your prose.

Remember that the metaphor is mechanical in the expression **geared to,** which will thus sound silly, as well as trite, in an inappropriate context: "The plan for the new highway was not *geared to* bicycles."

The phrases **general public** and **general consensus** are familiar redundancies that will puzzle you if you stop to think about them. When is *the public* or *a consensus* not *general?*

In titles like **attorney general** and **postmaster general,** *general* was originally understood to be not a noun but an adjective indicating a superior rank. But we are now more likely to think of *general* as the noun in these expressions. Plurals like *attorney generals* are far more common than niceties like *attorneys general.*

Perhaps because of its common use in computer jargon, the vivid and useful verb **generate** is in danger of becoming a cliché for *create* or *produce:* "The new campaign *strategy* is expected to generate support for the Democratic policy among upper-income groups." This technological sense of the word already appears to have supplanted the natural one of *procreate* or *engender:* "In the course of the summer, the hydrangea *generates* several large clusters of flowers."

Except in the conventional opening "ladies and gentlemen," the nouns **gentleman** and *lady* will appear cute, patronizing, and even facetious if used instead of man and woman.

Given is acceptable as a dangling modifier. See page 58.

Don't let clichés and colloquialisms beginning with **go** go by: "*go* by the boards, *go* down the drain, *go* for broke, *go* great guns, *go* to bat for, *go* to one's head, *go* to pieces, *go* off the deep end, *go* in for, *go* the distance, *go* down the tubes."

Gorgeous suggests a superficial beauty. In Shakespeare's *King Lear,* the suffering and mistreated King says to his cruel daughter: "Thou art a lady, if only to go warm were gorgeous."

A great many merely means *many*. And **greatly** should not be used to pump up deflated rhetoric: "I *greatly* admire your tireless patience and unflagging devotion."

The phrase **a growing number** has grown so old that it should be retired.

Hardly is followed by *when*, not *than:* "President Jefferson had *hardly* entered office when his administration was faced with a major scandal."

On the use of **he, he or she, his, hers,** and **his or hers** with personal pronouns, see Agreement, pages 45–46.

Health reasons is an awkward euphemism for illness: "He retired for health reasons." And a **heart condition** is a euphemism for *heart disease.* All hearts are in some condition, whether healthy or not.

Grammarians have long disputed the correctness of **cannot help but.** Some believe that it contains a double negative (*not . . . but*); others maintain that the construction is idiomatic. No consensus has been reached, and perhaps the dispute deserves to be put aside. If you wish to avoid using *cannot help but,* you may simply omit *but* and adopt the *-ing* form of the verb: "Priscilla *cannot help* being a fool."

On **hers, his, his or hers,** see Agreement, pages 45–46.

Home is best used not for a house in itself, but for a place of residence in relation to those who live there. Any place can be a *home* if it is considered the place one lives: a house, an apartment, a trailer, a ship. One can also say that some larger place is one's home: a village, a county, a country. When real estate agents advertise "an elegant home with a swimming pool and two acres," they are giving you the fast sell. *Homes* are not bought and sold, only houses.

The use of **hopefully** to mean *it is hoped* is both recent and widespread: "The new economic measures are expected to reduce spending, increase production, and, *hopefully,* to curb inflation." "You will receive the shipment, *hopefully,* next week." The objections to this use of *hopefully* are well known. Who is full of such hopes? The speaker? The subject of the sentence? Everyone? Doesn't *hopefully* mean *in a hopeful manner?* If you wish to avoid offending the fastidious, don't use the word in this way. But then, to be consistent, you should avoid other adverbs like *undoubtedly* which are used in the same way: "The new economic measures are *undoubtedly* expected to curb inflation." If you do use *hopefully,* use it with care, for its meaning is often closer to *perhaps* than to *it is hoped.* Remember then that *hopefully* may cast doubt upon the reliability of your statement. When you tell a client that shipment will arrive, *hopefully,* next week, you may cause your client to worry unnecessarily whether or not it will arrive on time.

However in the sense of *nevertheless* or *on the other hand* introduces a strong contrast. The placement of *however* in the sentence determines which parts of the sentence are to be contrasted, for the force of *however* falls on the words in front of it:

> The House approved the Taft-Hartley bill today. It voted down, *however*, the amendment proposed by Representative Clay.

> The House approved the Taft-Hartley bill today. The Senate, *however*, voted the measure down.

In the first example *however* points out a contrast between motions approved and rejected; in the second it points out a contrast between the House and the Senate. Many writers object to beginning a sentence with *however* because in the opening position *however* cannot point out the contrast specifically. Use *but* instead. It belongs at the beginning. Also remember that the adverb *however* is not a conjunction. It cannot join two clauses into a compound sentence without the help of a semicolon: "I like coffee; *however*, you like tea." Don't be confused by the subordinate conjunction *however*, which can both begin a sentence and join two clauses: "*However* the jury votes, I believe in your innocence." "Ruth always tried to win, *however* strong the odds were against her."

Don't let a prejudice against *me* lead you to use **I** as the object of a verb or of a preposition: "The court informed my lawyer and *me* (not *I*) that our appeal had been granted." "The contract had been signed by my partner and *me* (not *I*)." "The jury had assumed it to be *me* (not *I*) who had juggled the books." In each sentence the first-person pronoun must be *me*. In the first, the pronoun is the object of *informed;* in the second, the object of *by;* and in the third, the object of *assumed.*

Idea is often used merely to puff a phrase up with a specious intellectual dignity: "Most Americans are in favor of the *idea* of entering another war." Don't use the word, then, unless you mean to distinguish *idea* from practice. "Most Americans are in favor of the *idea* of a tax cut but would be disappointed by the results."

On the use of **i.e.,** see *e.g.,* page 105.

The phrases **if and when** and **immediately if not sooner** are contradictory and hackneyed.

Impact both as a noun (a synonym for *effect*) and as a verb (a synonym for *to affect*) is used so often by politicians and businessmen to describe the immediate and beneficial results of policy that its own *impact* has much diminished.

Implement is another innocent word made suspect by its use in bureaucratic prose. Try *carry out, put into effect, accomplish, fulfill.*

Writers have long confused **imply** and **infer.** *To imply* is *to suggest, to indicate indirectly:* "Mrs. Da Costa *implied* that she might resign." *To infer* is *to derive a conclusion from evidence.* "From her frequent remarks about how much she would like to live in Florida, I *inferred* that Mrs. Da Costa was planning to retire there."

Many prepositional phrases beginning with **in** may be replaced by simpler words: *in* addition to (*besides*); *in* advance of (*before*); *in* all probability (*probably*); *in* a manner similar to (*like*); *in* close proximity (*near*); *in* conjunction with (*with, together with*); *in* connection with (*from, by, about*); *in* excess of (*more than, over*); *in* height (*high, tall*); *in* length (*long*); *in* spite of the fact that (*although*); *in* view of the fact that (*since, because*); *in* terms of (*with, at, in, for*); *in* the course of (*during*); *in* the event that (*if*); *in* the near or not too distant future (*soon*); *in* the neighborhood of (*about, almost*). *In age, in size, in shape, in number,* and *in years* are usually altogether unnecessary.

Inasmuch as and **insofar as** often appear as windy substitutes for *because* or *since:* "*Inasmuch as* you have asked me to say a few words, I would like to begin by thanking my hosts." Reserve *inasmuch as* and *insofar as* for indicating degree or proportion: "I will help you inasmuch as I can."

The abstract noun **individual** refers to the person in contrast to the society, the state, or any corporate body: "We must zealously safeguard the rights of the *individual.*" Don't waste *individual* by using it to refer to a particular, though unidentified, person: "Officer Casey observed an *individual* (a man) in a green jumpsuit entering the drugstore."

Instance, like *case,* often leads to circumlocution: "In the *instance* of neighborhood service stations, the decontrol of oil prices may cause a sharp drop in profits." Here *in the instance of* simply means *for.*

An **intensive** course in Chinese compresses what might have been studied in five years into two. *Intensive* means *concentrated.* **Intense** means *strenuous, ardent, intent, difficult.* "Any course in Chinese, whether it lasted five years or two, might require *intense* study."

The words **interesting** and **interestingly** are unlikely to arouse the interest of any reader. Whenever you feel tempted to use them, reflect for a moment about what evokes your interest, and choose a more evocative word.

Involve is often a lazy writer's catchall: "He was arrested on charges *involving* (of) manslaughter and evading arrest." "The appointment of Klein as ambassador could *involve* (cause) a debate over his confirmation in the Senate." "The report *involves* (is about, concerns) the burning of Atlanta." When well used, *involve* suggests engagement, envelopment: "After years of research, Nicholas Merriam was wholly *involved* in the search for a vaccine."

114

The anticipatory constructions **it is** and **it was** can be used to emphasize the words that immediately follow them: "The police accused Johnson of the murder, but *it is* Thompson, not Johnson, who killed Dingley." Here **it is** stresses the name Thompson. But often writers use the construction merely to stall: "Air Europe welcomes your patronage. *It is* our concern (better, "We want") to offer you the safest and most comfortable service possible." Many stale formulas begin with *it is:* "*it is* with deep regret"; "*it is* with pleasure"; "*it is* my belief that." Avoid passive statements beginning *it is* unless the statement must be impersonal: "Little is known about Meckler. *It is* widely believed that she escaped to Mexico."

At this **juncture** is pretentious; it usually means no more than *now*. It can be used, however, to describe a dangerous concurrence of circumstances: "The battle for the Baltic Sea had been lost, and a heavy storm had disabled half the fleet. At this *juncture*, Admiral Ivanov was forced to return to port."

Just exactly and **just precisely** are redundant.

The noun **juvenile** is a legal term for a young defendant, a publishing term for a book written for children, and a theatrical term for an actor who plays youthful parts. In other contexts, the noun seems technical and cold when used instead of *child, young man,* or *young woman.*

Kind of and **sort of** as intensifiers meaning *somewhat* or *rather* are colloquial: "He's *sort of* nice." Plural phrases built upon *kind of, sort of,* and *type of* are subject to problems in agreement. In speech many people say "those *kind of* books" or "that *sort of* people." In formal writing the conflict between plural (*those, books, people*) and singular (*kind, sort*) can be jarring even though such phrases have appeared in the work of writers for centuries. The problem is easily avoided by consistency in number: "that *kind of* book," "those *kinds of* books," "that *sort of* person," "those *sorts of* people." If these solutions seem fussy, try "such people," "people like that."

Lack makes a poor understudy for the word you can't think of: "The entire population died of *lack* of food." The word lacking here is *starvation.* The *for* in *lack for* is superfluous: "The party *lacks (for)* support among the working class."

A large part, a large portion, a large number, and similar expressions of quantity are usually just overweight ways of saying *many* or *much.*

Lay is a transitive verb meaning *put down, put to rest:* "I *lay* the book on the table when my eyes get tired." *Laid* is both its past tense and its past participle: "I *laid* the book on the table when my eyes were tired." "I had *laid* the book on the table, but someone has taken it." *Lie* is an intransitive verb meaning *to be at rest:* "I *lie* in bed." Its past tense is *lay:* "I *lay* in bed all day." Its past participle is *lain:* "I could have *lain* in bed all day."

Don't use **level** unless you want to evoke a sense of hierarchy: "The board of directors believe the problem can be solved on an engineering *level.*" A clearer sentence would be: "The board of directors believe the problem can be solved by engineers."

Although **like** has long been used in speech and in print as a conjunction meaning *as* or *as if,* a strong prejudice prevails against this use in formal prose. In formal prose, use *like* as a preposition only: "The price of gasoline has risen *like* a gusher in a Saudi oil field." Note that the object of *like* is a noun, *gusher.* If a conjunction is required, use *as,* not *like:* "The price of gasoline has risen *as* I expected it to." Note that *as* is followed by an entire clause: a subject (*I*) and a predicate (*expected it to*). Don't avoid the mistake of using *like* for *as* only to fall into the opposite mistake of using *as* or *as with* for *like:* "Drugstore sales, *as with* (better, *like*) supermarket sales, have always been high for similar books." Sometimes a correct but obtrusive *as* clause can be replaced by a *like*-phrase: "Poland, *as is* (better, *like*) Czechoslovakia, is sometimes treated like a naughty child by the Soviet Union." Be careful not to leave a *like*-phrase dangling: "Like Homer, I believe Shaw had a keen sense of social satire." This sentence mistakenly likens its writer, not Shaw, to Homer.

Don't use **limited** as a euphemism for *small, few, rare, poor,* or *insufficient:* "My client is a person of *limited* means." Use *limited* only when limits are indeed applied: "The powers of the judge in a jury trial are *limited.*"

Avoid using **literally** merely for emphasis, as in "Foreign automobile manufacturers have *literally* declared war on Detroit." *In effect* or *virtually* would be more appropriate than *literally*, which literally means *word for word.*

Major is overused in the sense of *great* or *important.* Press releases and advertisements invite the public to see "a *major* motion picture" or hear "a *major* artist" perform a Beethoven piano concerto. Intellectuals strive to address the "*major* political issues" of the decade. Remember that *major* (which means *greater*) indicates a higher degree of importance or greatness: "Intellectuals today address many important issues, but the *major* issue, I believe, is the danger of nuclear war." Phrases such as *a major part, a major portion,* and *in a major way* can often be replaced by less cumbersome expressions: "I read a *major* portion (better, *most*) of the book." "Americans are influenced by television in a *major* way (better, *greatly influenced by*)." Similarly, **majority** is often used where *most* would serve equally well: "A *majority* of (better, *most*) Americans are influenced by television." A *majority* expresses no higher degree of statistical validity than *most* does.

117

For **male,** see **female,** page 108.

The word **manner** lends itself too readily to circumlocutions: "in a competent *manner*" (better, *competently*); "in a discourteous *manner*" (better, *discourteously*). "In the *manner* in which" can usually be replaced by *as:* "Behave towards others in the *manner in which* (better, *as*) you would like them to behave towards you." The tag phrase "in any way, manner, shape, or form" is pompous.

Marginal, often merely a word for *small, slight,* or *low,* can be used more effectively in describing something as lying on a tenuous dividing line, often one between success and failure: "Kennedy's victory was *marginal.*"

Massive is a cliché in the sense of *large scale* or *extensive.* Find a fresher word. "Mayor Miles Gerety, Jr. has called for a massive (better, *complete*) overhaul of the bus system." "The overhaul will require massive (better, *large, extraordinary*) capital expenditure."

For advice on the fearless use of **me,** see **I,** page 112 and **myself,** page 119.

Recently, **meaningful** has become one of the passwords of the near-intelligentsia, and it may be a long time before the word can be rehabilitated. Indeed *meaningful* was always a difficult word to use, since it is superfluous when applied to anything that has intrinsic meaning, like "a *meaningful* book."

By means of is often only a stuffy way to express *with* or *through:* "He opened the door by means of (better, *with*) a crowbar."

A measure of means little more than *some* or *certain:* "There was *a measure of* (better, *some*) disagreement over the bond issue."

Remember when using **more** that there are at least two parts to every comparison: "Apples are *more* nutritious than peppermints." Make clear what is being compared to what. Many advertisements deceptively leave the comparisons dangling: "Buy Redeye, the *more* nutritious apple." Be careful not to compare absolutes: *favorite* (not *more favorite*); *unique* (not *most unique*). And remember to form the comparative and superlative of compound adjectives like *well-liked* with *better* and *best: better-liked, best-liked.*

Psychologists and district attorneys concern themselves with what **motivates** people. Do groups or companies have **motivations?** "Gotty would like to find out what motivated Insco to acquire Undertel." Use *why* instead: "Gotty would like to find out *why* Insco acquired Undertel."

Do not let an unnatural fear of using *me* lead you into using **myself** instead. In the following sentence, for example, *me* is the appropriate pronoun: "The department chairman has asked Mrs. Brewster and *me* (not *myself*) to review his appointments." The verb *asked* takes a direct object, so that the objective form of the pronoun is used. *Myself* has only two uses: reflexive and intensive. *Myself* is used reflexively when the subject of the sentence and the object are the same: "I cut *myself*." The intensive *myself* is used for emphasis: "I *myself* like foreign cars." *Myself* is not appropriate in a comparison: "James is as mean as *myself* (better, *as I am*)." *Himself, herself, yourself, yourselves, ourselves,* and *themselves* have analogous reflexive and intensive uses.

Like *kind, sort,* and *type,* **nature** often leads a writer into vague writing: "He made remarks of an uncomplimentary *nature*." Instead, write: "He made uncomplimentary remarks," "He insulted," "He disparaged," "He found fault with."

In the near future and **in the not too distant future** are roundabout ways of saying *soon,* and **in the neighborhood of** is usually a clumsy way of saying *about.*

Negative and **affirmative** can lead to slippery or evasive responses: "My answer is in the *negative.*" "I have an *affirmative* answer on that." Let your yea be yea, and your nay, nay. *Negative* in the sense of *disagreeable* is often vague: "The *negative* effects of radiation are well known." Are these effects *harmful? deleterious? lethal?*

Although many writers will sometimes use *or* with *neither,* traditional standards call for **neither . . . nor:** "Neither rain nor snow deters the intrepid mail carrier." On the placement of *neither . . . nor,* see pages 71–72; on the number of the pronoun *neither,* see pages 43–44.

On problems of agreement with **nobody** and **no one,** see pages 45–46.

None may be either singular or plural: "*None* of the puppies has/have been vaccinated." Here the plural *have* is more common, for the sentence in effect states that all of the puppies have yet to be vaccinated. *None* is usually singular, however, when it emphasizes not what a group has in common, but what distinguishes one member from the group: "All of our staff physicians are excellent, but *none* of them is as popular as Dr. Peterson." *None* is always singular when it has the sense *no amount,* plural when it has the sense *no quantity:* "*None* of my effort was noticed; *none* of its effects were obvious." See Agreement, pages 45–46.

Place **not** in careful relation to *all* and *every.* A sentence like: "Not every joke in the book is funny" tells you that although some of the jokes in the book are funny, others are not. But "Every joke in the book is not funny" is ambiguous. It may have the same meaning as the first sentence, but it may mean that not a single joke is funny. In speech you could use your voice in order to show which interpretation you intended. In writing for the silent reader, however, it is best to choose the least ambiguous placement of *not*.

Not about to is colloquial for *not going to, does not intend to. Not all that, not that, not too* and *not so* are colloquial as intensifiers: "I am *not that* enthusiastic about the trip."

Objective is bureaucratic jargon for *purpose, aim,* or *object:* "The *objective* of the program is to raise the standard of living." If you use the term at all, observe a distinction between what an act is intended to accomplish (its object, aim, or purpose) and the target or goal of the act: "The *object* of the program is to raise the standard of living; its first *objective* will be the slums of New Orleans."

You are **obliged** to someone who has done you a favor; that is, you are figuratively in debt. But you are *obligated* (*required*) to pay your taxes.

Omitting a second **of** in a series may create ambiguity: "I demand the abolition of capital punishment and (of) the practice of forced labor." Unless the second *of* is used, the practice of forced labor becomes the second of the speaker's demands, rather than the second of the proposed abolitions.

For the use of a superfluous *a* in expressions like "kind **of** (a) house," see **a.**

The preposition **of** is unnecessary in constructions like: "a figure (of) between six and seven thousand"; "a cost (of) from five to ten million." The *of* in the colloquialism *off of* may stand out as similarly unnecessary when used in for-

121

mal writing: "The general climbed *off* (not *off of*) his horse."

Several phrases formed with **on** are usually long-winded. Instead of "*On* the basis of," write *on, by, after* or *because of.* "On the grounds that," can become *since* or *because.* "On the part of" can be replaced by *among* or *by.*

On the use of **one another,** see *each other.*

Restrict use of the adjective **operative** to contexts that suggest activity or efficiency: "Charles Lamb believed that a person should be not *operative,* but contemplative." The noun *operative* used to mean skilled worker, but now is more often used to denote a spy or undercover agent.

In scientific or technical contexts **optimum** is appropriate for describing the best one can attain under given circumstances: "The virus was cultured under optimum conditions." But don't use **optimum** merely as a substitute for *best.*

To **orient** something originally meant to point it towards the east, the Orient, but has come to mean to ascertain bearings or to set in position: "When you arrive in a new city you must *orient* yourself." *Orient* is also used for its vague sociological connotations. Academics describe Protestantism as a *work-oriented* religion and perhaps describe village society as *family-oriented.* **Orientate** is a ponderous substitute for *orient.*

Outside *the house* is more concise than *outside of the house.*

Owing to is acceptable as a dangling modifier (see page 58) but *owing to the fact that* is a circumlocution.

Reference to **parameters** should be left to mathematicians, who know what *parameters* are: constants used in describing a family of curves. Others who write of *parameters* usually show only a vague sense of what the word means and, perhaps through confusing the word with *perimeter,* use it as a sloppy metaphor for *limit* or *guideline,* as in the following sentence: "The council must first lay down some *parameters* to work under."

Particular is often slipped in to give an unneeded boost to *this* and *that:* at this (*particular*) time, on that (*particular*) day.

Legal contracts refer to *the* **party** *of the first part* and *the* **party** *of the second part;* telephone operators announce that they have *your party* on the line; and police officers report that they need assistance for *injured parties.* These impersonal uses of *party* are bureaucratic and commercial. In all other contexts, *person* is usually a better choice. If a more specific word can be found, use it: *man, woman, child.*

Pass away and *pass on* are maudlin euphemisms for *die.*

Past is redundant when used with words that in themselves describe something that has a past, such as *history, achievements, record,* or *experience.* In special circumstances, you may, however, need to distinguish a past record from a record yet to be attained.

The Latin preposition **per** (for) is found in many established and useful terms of measurement: *per diem, per annum, per capita,* miles *per* hour, revolutions *per* minute. In a non-technical context, a single *a(n)* will do the job: "I visit my brother three times *per* (better, *a*) year."

A **period** *of three years* is redundant; "three years" will serve alone. "A long period of time" is also redundant; say "a long time" or "a long period."

Personal and **personally** are often unneeded modifiers to words that by themselves describe personal qualities or actions: "Julio is a (personal) friend." "He has a (personal) preference for strawberry jam." "She shook hands with everyone (personally)." In the last example, *personally* is trying to do the job of *individually.*

Personnel is commonly used to describe the staff of a large organization: *government personnel, military personnel, corporate personnel.* As a collective noun, it can take either a singular or plural verb: "Library *personnel* are asked to attend a brief meeting at 11:00." But *personnel* sounds odd if it is made to stand in place of such plural nouns as *employees, people,* or *men:* "Fourteen army *personnel* were killed in the raid." See collective subjects, pages 44–45.

Don't write **plus** when all you mean is *and* or *besides:* "She is an excellent manager *plus* (better, *and*) a fine colleague." "The plan calls for too many sales representatives; *plus* (better, *besides*) the advertising budget is far too high."

Point of view often leads to circumlocution: "From the *point of view* of politics, the speech was a success." A better sentence would be: "The speech was politically successful." *Point of view* as a noun meaning *opinion* is usually unnecessary. Why not *view?* **This point in time** is a long phrase for *now.*

Precede means *go before:* "The introduction *precedes* the text." **Proceed** means *go forward:* "The division *proceeded* to Bastogne." Be careful about the spelling of these two words.

Prefer is normally followed by *to:* "Levine *prefers* modern dance to classical ballet." You cannot, however, use *to* with constructions requiring a second *to:* "I *prefer to* sing to to dance"; "I *prefer* to go to New Haven to New York." Instead, use *rather than:* "I *prefer to* sing *rather than* to dance." "I *prefer to* go to New Haven *rather than* to New

York." But do not use *than* when *to* will do: "Roderick *prefers* listening to Bach *than* (better, *to*) going out dancing."

Use *before* instead of **previous to** and **prior to.**

Principal is an adjective meaning *most important* or *first:* "The *principal* cause of failure is laziness." It is also a noun describing a person in a leading position: *a school principal,* or the *principal* in an orchestra. **Principle** is a noun describing a fundamental law or doctrine: "We must abide by the *principles* of international diplomacy."

As computers become more and more widely used, you are likely to find the word **program** more and more widely used. But most writers still reserve the verb *to program* to its technical context. Elsewhere it sounds mechanistic: "The accounting department is now *programmed* to handle all return orders."

Proportion gives rise to several shapeless circumlocutions: *a large proportion, a great proportion, in greater or larger proportion.* Try *most* or *more.*

Provided is an acceptable dangling modifier, but don't use it where a simple *if* will work: "I will come to the party *provided* (better, *if*) my car starts." Reserve *provided* for contexts where a provision is indeed being made: "*Provided* that Congress approves the funds, the program will start on time." *Provided* is preferred by most writers to *providing,* perhaps because it is less likely to be read as a dangling modifier.

Using the Latin **qua** for *as* is pedantic.

You can often make a sentence more succinct by eliminating the word **quality:** "His remarks had an introductory *quality.* Better: "His remarks were introductory."

125

A *large* **quantity,** *a similar* **quantity,** *a negligible* **quantity** are circumlocutions for *much, as much, little.*

Quite is often an unnecessary word that weakens, rather than strengthens your statement. Remember that in American usage, *quite* has two quite different senses—either *absolutely* or only *somewhat:* "I am *quite* (*absolutely*) opposed to gun control." "The sky was *quite* (*somewhat*) sunny." Used with *not, quite* always has the sense of *absolutely:* "I am *not quite* ready."

Quote is a verb: "I like to *quote* precedent to support my case." What you *quote* is a *quotation,* not a *quote:* "I will support my case with *quotations.*"

Be sure to invoke the geometric precision of **radius** only when necessary. In phrases like "residents who live within a ten mile *radius* of the city," *within ten miles* would suffice.

Re and **in re** are appropriate only to legal documents and memoranda.

Many verbs beginning with **re-** (*refer, regain, return, reply, report*) do not need the help of *back* or *again:* "Anna *referred* (back) to the book about Darwin."

Newton's second law of motion states that every action must have an equal and opposite **reaction.** Human beings have a greater range of response, and you should reflect this variety in your choice of words. Don't fall back on *react* and *reaction,* which sound impersonal and mechanical: "What is your *reaction* to the news of the Soviet invasion, Senator?" Better: "What do you think of the invasion, Senator?" "Jowett *reacted* badly to the news of his wife's death." Better: "Jowett *broke down* at the news of his wife's death." A dog can *react* to its master's call by coming home. But the master, in return, *replies* to the dog's bark, "I'm coming."

Real and **really** are overworked as intensifiers: "The problem is a *real* shortage of manpower." "We *really* need more men." Reserve these words for making a distinction between the real and the ideal.

The **reason** *is because* is redundant; *for the simple* **reason** is a cliché.

Have **reference to** is roundabout for *refer to.*

In **regard** *to, with* **regard** *to* and *as* **regards** can usually be pared down to *concerning, regarding,* or *about.* The *-less* in *regardless* means *without,* making *irregardless* a double negative.

Phrases like *in* **relation** *to,* **relative** *to, have* **relation,** and **relating** *to* can often be replaced by a simple preposition: "Jack has a good idea in *relation* to (better, *about*) the direct mail program." "My own opinion *relating* to (better, *of*) the program is well-known." The phrases are useful, however, when two or more things are indeed being related: "The sales figures must be studied in *relation* to the costs of advertising and promotion."

The distinction between **relation** and **relationship** is often blurred by writers who use *relationship* where *relation* will do: "The study will determine the *relationship* of promotion to sales." *Relationship* is unnecessary here because *relation* itself describes two things as being related. Reserve *relationship* for describing a specific kind or degree of relatedness between people. Most strictly used, *relationship* describes degree of kinship: "The genealogy does not show the *relationship* of John Harington of Stepney to John Harington of London." More loosely, *relationship* describes the quality of the social relations between two or more people who may or may not be kin: "I have a close relationship with Jack." Some might argue that even here *relationship* is perhaps superfluous: "I have close *relations* with Jack." All will agree that popular psychology has made *relationship* into a cliché but the danger here is that *relations* suggests sexual relations.

Respective and **respectively** are fussy and should be used only as a last resort to prevent confusion: "The chemistry department and the biology department will move to Welch Hall and King Hall, *respectively.*" But remember that you can often avoid using *respective(ly)* by rewriting: "The chemistry department will move to Welch Hall, and the biology department to King Hall." Never use *respective(ly)* when the context admits no possibility of confusion: "The Soviet ambassador and the French ambassador were notified of the change by their embassies."

With **respect** *to* and *in* **respect** *to* usually mean no more than *about* or *for,* which should be used instead: "The board made provisions *in respect to* (better, *for*) the possible illegality of the merger."

The legal use of **said** as an adjective meaning *mentioned previously* ("the *said* criminal") is inappropriate in contexts that do not demand such legal precision.

Using **same** to mean *it* or *them* gives the effect of antiquated commercial jargon: "The N.Y. office ordered seven gross of white gloves and paid for *same* (better, *them*) in cash.

Seeing as how is roundabout for *seeing that* or *because.*

Do not use **self** to mean *I* or *me:* "I wish to book seats for *self* and family on the 8:30 flight."

A recent American president described his secretary of state as "a senior-citizen-type statesman." He meant **senior,** but his mistake reflects the difficulty many writers have in finding an appropriate word for old people. *Elderly people* or *the elderly* is perhaps softer than *the old* or *old people,* but *senior citizen, senior persons,* and *seniors* are euphemisms.

In a _____ **sense** often appears as a circumlocution and is often used to add unneeded emphasis: "*In a real sense,* then, Laura brought new dignity to her office."

The *Oxford English Dictionary* cites Milton as the inventor of the word **sensuous.** Coleridge adopted Milton's particular use of the word, and the distinction that the two poets drew between *sensuous* and **sensual** is still jealously preserved. What belongs to the realm of the senses but is not gross or lascivious is *sensuous.* "Great poetry," wrote Milton, should be "simple, *sensuous,* and passionate." The grosser pleasures of the senses are merely *sensual:* "Venus and Adonis sported in *sensual* delight."

She is sometimes used incorrectly for *her:* "I know no one like *she (her)*"; "Mr. Onofrio willed his property to *she (her)* who was wearing the red dress at the funeral." See pages 52–53.

Don't use **sic** to be cute or snide. The word means *thus* or *yes* and should be reserved for occasions when you feel there is a clear danger of being misunderstood. Use it, for example, when you need to quote a passage that includes a misspelled word: "Adams wrote, 'I have no patients (sic) with such rudeness.'" But do not use *sic* when you quote a passage that makes a point you think silly or wrong.

Significant and **significantly** are so often used for emphasis that they mean little more than *great* and *greatly, important* and *importantly.* But something *significant* may not be important. A survey may produce *significant* results— results that are statistically valid and interpretable—but these results will not necessarily be of great importance.

129

Similar is an adjective meaning *resembling*. It cannot do the work of *the same* or of the preposition *like:* "Japan, *like* (not *similar to*) the United States, exports many of its automobiles."

Situation can often be omitted: "The army was in a dangerous situation (better, *in danger*)." "We are in a problem *situation* with our personnel department." Better: "We have problems in our personnel department."

In informal writing **so** is a common intensifier: "This book is *so* good." In more formal contexts reserve *so* for indicating the connection between a quality and its effect: "This book is *so* good *that* I could not put it down."

On the use of **somebody** and **someone,** see pages 45–46.

On **sort,** see **kind.**

Saying **state** when you mean *say* is pretentious. Can you imagine *stating* hello? To *state* something is *to declare it formally or fully:* "In his speech before the curia, Pope Innocent III *stated* that he approved of the concordat with the emperor." "Cynthia *stated* her opposition to my plans."

The verb **structure** and its attendant adjective **structured** are overused, perhaps because they seem to have sociological authority: "John functions best in a highly *structured* environment." Better: "John works best where he knows what is expected of him."

Such, like *same,* should not be used as a personal pronoun meaning *them* or *those:* "I purchased two batteries and returned *such* (better, *them*) to the company because they were defective."

Terminate has become a euphemism for describing several kinds of unpleasant departures or separations. Marriages *terminate* in divorce, and employees are *terminated* when they are no longer needed.

Franklin Roosevelt's last words are reported to have been "I have a **terrific** headache." Did he mean that he felt mortal terror or that he had an unusually intense pain? In formal prose, *terrific(ally)* and *terrible* (*terribly*) are best used for what does indeed put the writer in terror.

When a noun follows **than** it may be either subjective or objective, depending upon the context:

> Flagstad sang better *than* Nilsson sings.
> Flagstad sang Wagner better *than* she sang Glück.

The noun following *than* is either the object of a verb (she sang Glück) or the subject (Nilsson sings). Omitting the whole clause except for the noun can create an ambiguity: "I admire John more than Jane." Do I admire John more than Jane admires him, or do I admire John more than I admire Jane? When a pronoun follows the *than,* attention to the case of the pronoun should prevent any misunderstanding:

> I admire him more *than* her.
> I admire him more *than* she.

But so many writers have fallen into the bad habit of using the objective *her* instead of the nominative *she* that to be certain of avoiding ambiguity, you may have to make the statement in full: "I admire him more *than* she admires him."

When you use **that** as an intensifier, the effect is folksy, not formal: "The report is not *that* well researched." Better: "The report is not very well researched," or simply, "The report is not well researched."

The conjunction **that** is often superfluous and can be omitted from many sentences, especially short ones. No one misses *that* in the following sentence: "Chicken Little said (*that*) the sky was falling." But the rhythm of a longer sentence may make you wish to retain a *that:* "The Senator decided *that* the votes to be won through a television debate with his opponent would justify the risk." In other sentences, retaining a well placed *that* will prevent misunderstanding: "Mrs. James said (*that*) on Wednesday (*that*) she would submit her resignation." Is Wednesday the day of her announcement or the day of her resignation? Retaining one of the *thats* and striking the other would make the timing clear.

On the distinction between the relative pronouns **that** and **which,** see pages 64–67.

On **their** and **they** used with *everyone, everybody,* see pages 45–46.

Most people will recognize the form **theirselves,** but never use it *themselves.*

On the sparing use of **therefore,** see page 14.

On **these kind, these sort, these type, those kind,** etc., see *kind of* and *sort of,* page 115.

On the use of **this** with only a vague reference, see page 50.

The metaphor **time frame** usually can be replaced by an everyday adverb: "in this *time frame*" (better, *now*), "in that *time frame*" (better, *by then, tomorrow, at that time*).

To all intents and purposes is a tedious way to say *in effect.*

Together with is often merely redundant for *and.* "Jack (*together*) *with* Jill, climbed up the hill."

The use of **top** to mean *principal, foremost, best,* or *greatest* is colloquial or informal. In this sense, *top* has no place in serious writing: "The experiment was conducted at one of the *top* laboratories on the West Coast."

A country lane that winds about is **tortuous,** or *twisty;* riding on that lane on a foggy night could be *torturous,* or *a torture.*

Reserve **total** and **totally** for what can be added up into a sum, or at least for something that is a whole: "He invested his *total* savings in the car." "The investment was a *total* loss." The words are inappropriate when they simply mean *in every way* or *very:* "He *totally* enjoyed his new car." "The ride was *totally* enjoyable."

Bring some peace to your writing by finding substitutes for **trigger:** "The walk-out was *triggered* by the management's refusal to raise the retirement benefits." Try *start, begin, set off, cause, incite.*

You may **try and do** something in speech, but *try* **to** *do* it in writing. The *try and* construction may offend some readers, and there is no reason to insist upon it except to imitate the patterns of everyday speech.

The phrase **type of** can usually be omitted: "She is a brilliant (*type of*) person." "This is an intellectual (*type of*) journal." Reserve *type* for technical distinctions: "*type of* blood," "*type of* engine."

Undue, unduly, unnecessary, and **unwarranted** sometimes lead a writer into truisms: "There is no need for *undue* concern."

The distinction between **unique** and *rare* is worth preserving: "Great cities are *rare,* but Paris is *unique.*" *Unique* does not admit comparison. Great cities can be less *rare* than great men, but Paris can be no more or less *unique* than Rome. *Unique* means *one of a kind.*

On using **us** and the other objective forms of the pronouns, see pages 52–54.

Usage is a customary or conventional use. This book is about English *usage*. Another book might describe the **usages** of the Roman Catholic church. Don't use *usage* where **use** will do. **Utilization** and **utilize** are often abused in the same way. Usually they are just long ways of saying *use:* "Only ten percent of all commuters utilize (better, *use, ride*) the bus." Reserve *utilize* to mean *use to advantage* or *profit from use of:* "We must *utilize* all our natural resources."

Avoid using **various** as a pronoun: "*Various* (better, *some, several*) of the cultures were contaminated."

Common intensifiers like **very,** *quite, almost,* and *somewhat* tend to ring false in prose: "The campaign was *very* reminiscent of her earlier attempts to get into office." Although in speaking the sentence aloud you could give conviction to *very* by your tone of voice, the written word *very* betrays a lack of confidence. Substituting a more sophisticated intensifier will only mask the problem: "The campaign was *highly* reminiscent" or "*extremely* reminiscent." Let your adjective or adverb stand on its own.

Viable derives from the Latin *vita* (life) and means *able to live, grow, or develop:* "It is not clear at this stage that the fetus is *viable*." The cliché *viable alternative* indicates an opportunity or second choice that the writer thinks stronger or more practicable. *Alternative* alone will usually suffice, or substitute such words as *choice, opportunity,* or *preference.*

Remember that adjectives formed with **well** like *well-read, well-turned,* and *well-thumbed* form their comparatives and superlatives with *better* and *best,* not *more* and *most: well-read, better-read, best-read.*

Where refers to place, and makes an illogical stand-in for *when* or *if:* "Flynn tried to call each of his supporters, and, *where* (better, *if*) he was unable to reach them, sent them a letter of thanks." *Where* can be used with *from*, as in "I asked *where* he will be coming *from*," but not with *at* or *to*.

On the possible differentiation of **which** and **that,** see pages 64–67.

Because the conjunction **while** has a strong temporal sense (*during the time that, at the same time as*), using it in place of *although* can be confusing: "*While* I arrived on Tuesday, Celia arrived on Monday." You may be tempted to use *while* because you don't want a conjunction as strong as *although*. But why not drop the conjunction altogether? "I arrived on Tuesday; Celia arrived on Monday."

At the end of the eighteenth century Noah Webster scoffed at the scrupulous use of **whom.** Today few would find fault with a phrase like "the person *who* I spoke to." Directly after a preposition, however, all writers still prefer *whom:* "the person to *whom* I spoke," "the person of *whom* we spoke." Using *whom* when *who* is needed shows false learning: "Martina is a candidate *who* (not *whom*) I thought was worthy of my support." *Who* is correct here, since the pronoun acts as the subject of the verb *was:* "*who was* worthy."

Do not be afraid to use **whose** to mean *of which;* no one will think that you are personifying a thing. You avoid the awkwardness that *of which* usually brings: "Grosvenor was president of an international corporation whose profits (not, *of which the profits*) are about six million a year."

Several circumlocutions begin with **with:** "*with* reference to," "*with* regard to," "*with* respect to." In these three cases, it is better to use *about.* Instead of "*with* the exception of," say *except* or *except for*. *With* is also used with a participial phrase as a lazy substitute for clear syntactic connection: "Baseball is the most popular sport, *with* tennis catching up to it quickly." Rewrite to indicate the relation more clearly: "Baseball is the *most* popular sport, although tennis is quickly catching up to it."

Would can be used to show that an action is habitual or repeated: "Morris *would* arrive at the office unshaven." But when another word or phrase, like *always* or *every Tuesday*, conveys the sense that the action is usual, *would* is unnecessary: "Morris *always* arrived at the office unshaven." *Would* can also be used to express possibility or contingency: "The doctor *would* see you today, if he had free time."

On the use of **you** as a pronoun meaning *one*, see pages 55–56. On **yourself,** see **myself,** page 119.

PART IV

———————— ♦ ————————

PUNCTUATION
AND
TYPOGRAPHY

11

Punctuation Marks

Punctuation guides both the voice and the eye. Some of our punctuation marks were first devised in the Middle Ages to indicate to those chanting the liturgy when to pause for breath and whether to let their voices rise or fall before the pause. Modern punctuation still influences the cadence or intonation of the words on a page:

> She's here. She's here? She's here!

Other elements of our punctuation system grew out of the scribes' and printers' desire to mark not musical phrasing, but syntactical phrases. Commas, for example, came into use in England in the 1520s, in imitation of the practice of European printing houses. Printers used commas to make clear to readers' eyes the units of syntax within a sentence. General use of modern quotation marks, to distinguish between the author's own words and the words of another, dates only from the eighteenth century.

Punctuation is at once the most conventional and the most idiosyncratic of the activities involved in writing. Rules guide the appropriate placement of marks and points. These rules may vary slightly from one profession or publication to another, but no writer can punctuate without them. A sense of how sentences should look and how they should sound, even to the silent reader, will affect how you punctuate. Since this sense always involves mediating between what language demands of the writer and what the writer demands of language, punctuation exposes in its incidental way the whole point of writing.

The Apostrophe

The apostrophe marks the omission of letters or numerals: *it's* (it is), *don't* (do not), *four o'clock* (of the clock), *Class of '80* (1980).

The possessive of most singular nouns is formed by adding *'s* and of most plural nouns by adding *'*: *Mrs. Pankhurst's, Chicago's, states'*. For the possessives of nouns ending in *s* and other anomalies, see *Possessives*, pages 158–159.

No apostrophe is used in possessive pronouns: *its, hers, his, ours, yours, theirs*.

The plural of some compound words and phrases requires an apostrophe, especially when the last element of the compound is not a noun: *thank-you's, chin-up's*.

The apostrophe should also be used to indicate plural forms of symbols, abbreviations, characters, and numerals: *Δ's, r.p.m.'s, p's and q's, counting by 5's; during the '60s*. Note that the style used by many publishers drops the apostrophe both before and after the numerals denoting a decade: *the 60s, the 1960s*.

The Colon

Colon derives from the Greek word *kolon* meaning limb. Colons always mark off a limb from a body, as, for example, the salutation from the body of a formal letter: *Dear Senator:*

Colons mark off a categorical statement from its reformulation:

> Professor Wright found that criticism of Yang-ti
> was widespread: local oral traditions, performances
> by wandering dramatic troupes, and eventually
> even stories and novels conventionally depicted him
> as a bad ruler.

They may also signal the amplification of a statement, especially by specific examples:

> He was criticized for ordering many extravagant
> new constructions: palaces, gardens, carriages, and
> boats.

In introducing a list, the phrases *as follows* and *the following* require a colon, but not all lists require these phrases:

> The Han historians denounced Yang-ti for exhib-
> iting all of the following vices: favoritism, corrup-
> tion, licentiousness, and lack of respect to ancestors.

Many vices would be less stiff than *all of the following vices,* and perhaps better still would be to eliminate the phrase and the colon altogether: "The Han historians denounced Yang-ti for exhibiting favoritism, corruption, licentiousness, and lack of respect to ancestors."

Colons are often more appropriate than commas in presenting quotations, especially when the quotation is lengthy enough to require indentation. See *Quotation Marks,* pages 152–153.

Colons have an official look, appropriate more to the business report than to the personal note, more to presenting a substantial excerpt than to introducing a snatch of conversation. The frequent use of them is distracting, disposing the reader to think of discontinuities rather than of continuity, to see limbs where there might be a whole body.

The Comma

The comma is certainly the most common punctuation mark and yet perhaps the most difficult to use. The refinements of using the comma often come down to a writer's preference or a publisher's style. But the most important uses of the comma are governed by conventions that no writer can safely ignore.

Commas with Compound Constructions

Use a comma before coordinate conjunctions (*and, but, or, nor, for, yet*) that join two independent clauses (each of which could stand as a sentence) into one compound sentence:

> The *Mayflower* had set sail for Virginia, *but* it dropped anchor in Massachusetts Bay.

> Myles Standish hoped to marry Priscilla Mullens, *and* John Alden spoke to her on his behalf.

The comma signals the separation of the two clauses. In the second example, the comma prevents the reader from getting off to a false start: "Myles Standish hoped to marry Priscilla Mullens and John Alden. . . ." The comma before the conjunction may be omitted in very short compound sentences:

> Love it or leave it.

> Will she or won't she?

Two independent clauses being joined by conjunctive adverbs (*thus, therefore, however, furthermore*) must be marked with a semicolon, not a comma. See *Semicolon,* pages 150–151.

> The efficiency of the engine has increased; *thus* the new manifold must be working properly.

Note that no comma is necessary when two dependent clauses (neither of which could properly stand as a sentence) are being joined:

> When his settlement in Newfoundland failed *and* (when) an extensive territory north of the Potomac became available, Lord Baltimore petitioned the King for a new grant. He trusted that his farmers would prosper from the longer growing season *and* (that) his shepherds would benefit from the less rocky terrain.

In both of these sentences a comma before the *and* would confuse rather than clarify. In the first, both "his settlement . . . failed" and "an extensive territory . . . became available" are dependent on *when*. In the second, both the prosperity of the farmers and the benefits to the shepherds are what Lord Baltimore trusted in.

Commas with Series

Two compound nouns, verbs, adjectives, or adverbs are not normally marked by a comma: *beautiful and free, quickly and easily, came and went*. But when there are three or more compounded elements, a series is established.

Separate the members of a series with commas:

> Einstein questioned the concepts of absolute space, absolute time, and absolute velocity.

Omitting the last comma, as many journalists do, could cause a momentary confusion:

> The suspect has been charged with shoplifting, resisting arrest, and assault.

The last comma will tell the reader immediately that assault is a third charge and not the object of resisting.

A series of adjectives may sometimes pose special problems.

143

> Friar Lawrence seems a kind, considerate, godly
> clergyman.

These adjectives, separated by commas, all modify clergy-man. The status of the adjectives is equal. You could even put them in a different order without disrupting the sense or changing the punctuation:

> Friar Lawrence seems a godly, kind, considerate
> clergyman.

You could also join the adjectives with and: *kind and considerate and godly.*

Adjectives do not always have equal status.

> Wole Soyinka is a famous African playwright.

Here *African* modifies *playwright,* but *famous* modifies *African playwright.* You could not change the order of the adjectives: *African famous playwright.* And you would not join the adjectives with *and: famous and African.* Because *African playwright* makes a verbal unit and *famous* acts as if it were a single adjective modifying *African playwright,* no comma is necessary here. No matter how many adjectives appear in front of a noun, no comma is necessary if the whole phrase—noun and adjectives—constitutes a verbal unit:

> Harriet wore her brother's smelly old tweed jacket.

Commas with Supplementary Modifiers
and Introductory Phrases

Supplementary modifiers are always set off by a pair of commas:

> The senator, who was recently convicted of graft,
> refuses to resign.

Failure to set off the supplementary modifier with commas might change the meaning of the sentence. In this example, omission of the commas would suggest that there was more than one member of the Senate who was refusing to resign. For a full discussion of *Necessary and Supplementary Modifiers*, see pages 63–67.

Other kinds of incidental expressions also require a pair of commas:

> The rain will last, according to the Weather
> Bureau, for the whole week.

Leaving out the second comma of the pair can be bewildering:

> The rain will last, according to my husband for the
> whole week.

Using commas to set off introductory phrases or clauses is often a matter of style or preference. Some writers like to set off all such phrases:

> In desperation, Lincoln summoned McClellan to his
> office.

Some writers always set off dates with commas.

> In July, Lincoln summoned McClellan to his office.

Others do not think it necessary to place a comma after short introductory phrases. You should, however, set off with a comma any introductory participial phrase (verb + ing) or any construction that stands apart syntactically from the sentence that follows it:

> Coming into town, we recognized the old church
> immediately.

This being the case, we had to stop.

The service having just concluded, the rector was coming out the door.

Because the sun was in his eyes, he could not see us coming across the lawn.

Commas with Quotation Marks

Quotations of complete sentences introduced by attributive verbs like *say* or *write* are usually set off by a comma. The comma separates the quotation from the attributive phrase:

In this scene Hamlet tells the Player, "Speak the speech . . . trippingly on the tongue."

If the attributive phrase comes at the end of sentence, the comma is slipped in before the closing quotation mark:

"Speak the speech . . . trippingly on the tongue," Hamlet tells the Player.

When the attributive phrase is interpolated into the middle of the quoted sentence, you need two commas, one before and one after the attributive phrase:

"Speak the speech," Hamlet tells the Player, "trippingly on the tongue."

The comma is unnecessary if *that* is used with the attributive phrase:

Hamlet tells the Player *that* he should "speak the speech . . . trippingly on the tongue."

The comma is also unnecessary if less than a full sentence is being quoted:

> Hamlet remarks that the speech should be spoken
> "trippingly on the tongue."

When a quotation of three or more lines in length is indented from the body of the text, use a colon rather than a comma after the attributive phrase. See *Colon,* pages 140–141, and *Quotation Marks,* pages 152–153.

The Dash

Although dashes look like extended hyphens, they are really more closely related to commas, parentheses, and colons.

Like commas, dashes may be used in pairs to set off a phrase or clause in apposition. The dash, however, suggests some discontinuity between the words in apposition:

> McKim and White—the architects who had been
> put in charge of the Boston Public Library proj-
> ect—met Sargent on his visit to Newport in 1886.

Like a pair of parentheses—dashes like those above— may interrupt a sentence, especially to mark a change of context.

> Sargent worked for two years on the portrait—now
> held by the Tate Gallery—before submitting it to
> the jury at the Royal Academy.

The dash has other uses as well. It can introduce a short list in place of a colon, or suggest surprise, inconsistency, or incoherence.

The Exclamation Mark

Watch out for exclamation marks! Too frequent use of them marks your writing as immature. For the placement of exclamation marks with regard to quotations, see *Quotation Marks,* pages 152–153.

The Hyphen

Hyphens mark a partition, falling between syllables of a divided word (as at the end of a line of type) or between the elements of a compound word: *a blue-green glaze; nineteenth- and early twentieth-century poetry; a 250-ml beaker; an open-and-shut case.* Note that certain words become compounds and require the hyphen when used as adjectives, adverbs, and verbs, but not when used as nouns: *the twentieth century,* but *twentieth-century poetry; X rays,* but *X-rayed* and *X-ray technician.*

Many newly compounded words include a hyphen whereas familiar compounds do not: *railroad, foothill, bridegroom, guideline.*

Normally no hyphen is needed between a prefix and a stem word, but when the prefix ends and the stem begins with distinctly sounded vowels, add the hyphen: *re-elect.* When the vowels are nearly elided in a word as in the case of co-operate and pre-eminent, you may omit the hyphen: *cooperate, preeminent.*

Prefixes that do not derive from Latin or Greek, or are four or more letters long, or are unusual may require a hyphen: half-serious; semi-delirious; self-conscious. All of these words, especially self-conscious, are often written without hyphens. Readers demand only consistency and perhaps foresight in your usage. If you write *self-conscious* at the top of the page, do you not have to write *unself-conscious* at the bottom? And if *unself-conscious* (conscious of the unself?) seems absurd, *un-self-conscious* would be worse. Starting off with *selfconscious* would at least allow you to be *unselfconscious* about hyphens later.

Parentheses and Brackets

Use parentheses to set off commentary, supplementary information, or translation:

When she arrived in Phoenix (the rest of the family
had moved there while she was at college), Milly
found her parents' health considerably worse.

Anne of Austria (1601–1666) acted as regent of
France until Louis XIV came of age.

In the *Laws*, Plato considers *nous* (intelligence, reason) as the prime virtue.

Avoid frequent or extended parenthetical asides.
Truly extraneous material should be relegated to footnotes
or simply left out.

Use square brackets to indicate editorial interpola-
tions into quoted material:

Wordsworth writes of Michael's bereaved father:
"[he] never lifted up a single stone."

Altgeld reflected, "The Haymarket Square riots
[1886] brought me notoriety first and celebrity
later."

The Period

A period marks the end of a declarative sentence or an
expression standing for a sentence:

Last Friday, we drove into the city at rush hour.
Never again.

Use a period after abbreviations and certain contractions:

William K. Wimsatt, Jr., Ph.D., b. 1907, d. 1975,
Sterling Prof. of English, Yale Univ.

Many printers and editors omit the period after abbreviations. Usage varies from one profession or office to another. Consult the appropriate manual of style, and be
consistent.

Three spaced periods indicate the omission of words from a quotation; a fourth period is necessary if the omission extends to the end of the sentence:

> Blackmur writes, "Mr. Eliot's poetry is not devotional in any sense of which we have been speaking, but for the outsider—and we are all outsiders when we speak of poetry—it is the more religious for that."

> Blackmur writes, "Mr. Eliot's poetry is not devotional in any sense of which we have been speaking, but . . . it is the more religious for that."

> Blackmur writes, "Mr. Eliot's poetry is not devotional in any sense of which we have been speaking . . . ."

When quoting poetry, indicate the omission of one or more complete lines by a full line of spaced periods:

> Friends, Romans, countrymen, lend me your ears;
> I come to bury Caesar, not to praise him.
> . . . .
> I speak not to disprove what Brutus spoke,
> But here I am to speak what I do know.

The Semicolon

Use a semicolon to join two related sentences in the absence of a conjunction:

> Montessori questioned theories of education based on the experience of adults; her own method grew out of observing how children learn.

This arrangement is especially effective when the two sentences are parallel in structure:

> To the west stood a grove of beeches; to the east lay an ornamental lake.

A comma may replace the semicolon when both of the sentences are short:

Man proposes, God disposes.

When conjunctive adverbs such as *therefore, thus, moreover, furthermore,* and *however* are used to join sentences, use a semicolon, not a comma:

The authors of the study failed to measure the level of serum electrolytes in the control group; *thus* their conclusions are not to be considered reliable.

Rilke resided in Paris with his wife Clara from 1902 until the beginning of the war; *however,* he spent much of that time traveling abroad.

In lists, use a semicolon to separate items that themselves include commas:

Three of Henry VIII's wives were named Catherine: Catherine of Aragon, the mother of Princess Mary; Catherine Howard, the niece of the Duke of Norfolk; and Catherine Parr, the wife who survived him.

The Question Mark

Place a question mark at the end of a question that is asked directly or quoted exactly, but not at the end of a question that is summarized or reworded.

Who's on first?

He asked, "Who's on first?"

He asked me who was on first.

In business correspondence, a request put courteously in the form of a question does not require a question mark.

Will you please accept this gift with our compliments.

Would you kindly come in and settle your account as soon as possible.

Quotation Marks

Place quotation marks before and after transcriptions of speech or excerpts from printed works when you are preserving the exact wording of the original:

The Duke of Wellington called George III's sons "the damndest millstones about the neck of any government that can be imagined."

No quotation marks are necessary when the speech or source is being summarized in other words. Similarly, no quotation marks are necessary surrounding an extended quotation (of three or more lines in length) that is indented from the body of the text.

In American usage, commas and periods are placed within the closing quotation marks, whether or not those commas and periods appeared there in the original. Colons and semicolons are placed outside the closing quotation marks. Exclamation marks and question marks should be placed inside when they belong to the original material, outside when they do not.

In a brief "aside," the President criticized the reporters for their coverage of his recent trip to China.

George Eliot wrote of the novelist's moral obligation to depict the people who have done "the rough work of the world."

A group of Satie's most talented admirers came to be known as *"Les Six"*: Auric, Durey, Honegger, Milhaud, Poulenc, and Tailleferre.

On what grounds does the district attorney justify
calling him "a hardened criminal"?

"How can you call him that?" I asked.

Enclose in quotation marks the titles of poems, articles in periodicals, and songs:

"Among School Children," "A Look at Elementary
Education in the Soviet Union Today," "Be True to
Your School"

On occasion you might use quotation marks to disclaim responsibility for a phrase or to cast doubt upon the propriety of its use by others:

These "patriots" have succeeded only in slinging
mud upon the reputations of some of this country's
most prominent citizens.

12

Typography
and Possessives

— ◆ —

Capital Letters

Capitalize the initial letter of the first word of a sentence, an expression standing for a sentence, a direct quotation, or a line of verse (if capitalized in the original):

> Will the governor reconsider her decision? Possibly not.
>
> He asked, "What are your plans for the summer?"
>
> Come live with me, and be my love,
> And we will all the pleasures prove . . .

When citing the title of a book, article, or work of art, capitalize the initial letter of the first word and of all subsequent words except the articles, *a, an,* and *the* and any preposition or conjunction three letters or less in length:

> *Lives of the English Poets, Life with Father*

In scientific and scholarly bibliographies, practice differs. Consult the appropriate manual of style. For titles in foreign languages, conform to the typography in the source:

A l'ombre des jeunes filles en fleurs

Die schöne Müllerin

The proper names of a person or a group of people and the titles of respect or epithets applied to them should also be capitalized:

Doctor Jonas Salk, Queen Liliuokalani, Blind
Lemon Jefferson, the Amish, the International
Ladies' Garment Workers Union

For foreign names, conform to the usage of the original language:

Walter von der Vogelweide, Francisco de Goya y
Lucientes, Cathleen ni Houlihan

When an object or an abstract idea is treated as person, capitalize the name:

Nature (but in its natural setting); Spring poured
forth her bounty (an early spring).

Capitalize the names of specific places, peoples and languages:

Upper Newton Falls, New South Wales, Dade
County, The Euganean Hills, The Lake District,
Tagalog, Serbo-Croatian, Uranus, Betelgeuse (but
normally earth, sun, moon).

Capitalize also the adjectives derived from these names:

a Southerner, Southern cooking

Italics and Underlining

Although at one time printers gave special typographical emphasis to all names and titles, today such emphasis is reserved for a few classes of words, indicated on a printed page by italic or boldface type and on a typewritten page by underlining.

Underline or italicize the titles of books, periodicals, law cases, plays, or any work substantial enough to be printed as a separate volume:

> *The Death of the Heart, Diseases of the Kidney, Murder in the Cathedral*

Note that the names of sacred books are not underlined or italicized:

> Bible, Koran, Talmud, Vedas

The proper names of large works of art and means of transportation are also underlined or italicized:

> *The Polish Rider, Titanic, Spirit of St. Louis*

The titles of short pieces such as lyric poems, stories, and articles should be enclosed in quotation marks. See *Quotation Marks*, pages 152–153.

Underline or italicize those phrases borrowed from foreign languages that are pronounced (however approximately) as in their original language and are regarded as technical or untranslatable in meaning:

> *habeas corpus, trompe l'oeil, ex officio, allegro assai*

Use underlining or italics to call attention to words being considered as words and letters being considered as letters:

Tarragon derives from a Greek word meaning *dragon.*

Most German words beginning with the letter *c* are adoptions from other languages.

Possessives

To form the possessive of nouns, singular or plural, that do not end in an *s* or *z* sound, add an apostrophe followed by an *s* (*'s*):

child's play, children's games, Whistler's Mother, Descartes's theorems

Similarly, use an apostrophe followed by an *s* (*'s*) to form the possessive of most singular nouns ending in an *s* or *z* sound:

the bus's schedule, the *Daily News*'s editorials, Charles James Fox's speeches, Alice James's diaries, Wallace Stevens's poems

There are notable exceptions to this pattern. In certain stock phrases the apostrophe alone is used to form the possessive of singular nouns ending in an *s* or *z* sound: for *goodness'* sake. Biblical, classical, and foreign names are also exceptions: *Jesus', Moses', Aeneas'.* Note, however, that some classical names of only one syllable do require the apostrophe followed by an *s: Mars's.*

Form the possessive of plural nouns ending in an *s* or *z* sound by adding an apostrophe only:

lions' den, foxes' holes, the Jameses' house

The possessive of nouns joined by *and* is formed only on the last noun when possession is held jointly, but on all nouns in the series when possession is held individually:

> He first read Wordsworth's and Coleridge's poems
> in Wordsworth and Coleridge's *Lyrical Ballads.*

The poems were, of course, composed independently, but they were published together in a single venture.

The possessive of nouns joined by *or* is formed on all nouns in the series:

> Was the manuscript in Wordsworth's or Coleridge's handwriting?

Indicate the possessive of nouns in apposition on the last noun of the construction:

> at cousin Becky's apartment
>
> in my legal advisor Mrs. Gulbenkian's opinion
>
> in Mrs. Gulbenkian, my legal advisor's opinion

This last construction, clear in speech, is clumsy on the page and should be avoided.

The possessive of abbreviations and symbols is formed by adding an apostrophe followed by an *s* (*'s*):

> the F.B.I.'s files; the Δ's value

No apostrophe is used in the possessive pronouns *hers, his, its, ours, yours,* and *theirs.* Be especially careful to distinguish the possessive pronoun *its* from the contraction *it's,* meaning *it is.*

— ♦ —

CHAPTER

13

Documentation
of Sources

— ♦ —

Purposes

More than any other step in preparing a manuscript, the documentation of sources expresses the writer's connections to a community of other writers and readers. Documenting these references serves two purposes. It gives your readers all the information they need to find the material you consulted. And acknowledging how your work depends on the work that came before it (even your own previous work) helps readers to identify you as a responsible member of this community. It is incumbent upon you to acknowledge not just direct quotation, but also summary, paraphrase, and adaptation of other works. Even advice given in the course of editing the drafts of the essay needs to be acknowledged.

Giving information about your sources in a standard arrangement makes it easier for your readers to find even obscure material. Many professional groups and the editors of many publications have developed their own systems of documentation, as have some universities and corporations. Among the most widely used systems are those described in the Modern Language Association *Handbook for Writers of Research Papers, Theses, and Dissertations,* The Council of Biology Editors *Style Manual,* The Engineers Joint Council *Recommended Practice for Style of References in Engineering Publications,* The American Psychological Association *Publication Manual,* and The University of Chicago *Manual of Style.*

In the absence of specific guidelines from your editor or instructor, you should adopt one of the two most common systems of documentation. The first is used traditionally in academic publications in the humanities and in publications for general audiences. The second is used in publications in the social and natural sciences and in many corporate publications. Both systems are currently undergoing revision, so that in a few years there may be a greater similarity between them. You should consult with your editor or instructor at regular intervals about changes in the system you adopt.

Traditional Documentation

The traditional system for documentation in the humanities (adapted here from the 1977 *MLA Handbook*) indicates with asterisks or consecutively numbered superscripts the portion of the text requiring acknowledgment and places the documentation in footnotes (at the bottom of the relevant page of the text) or endnotes (on the last page of the text). At the end of the text (following any endnotes) there is generally a bibliography (list of works cited). The first reference to any published source should contain complete bibliographic information. Subsequent references may be briefer.

For first footnote or endnote references to books, use the following standard format:

the author's name, first name first

where relevant, the title of the section or chapter of the book, in quotation marks the title of the book, underlined or italicized

the name of the editor or translator (if any), first name first, preceded by "ed." or "trans."

the edition of the book you are using, if the title page indicates that it is not the first edition

in parentheses, the place of publication, followed by a colon, the name of the publishing company, followed by a comma, and the year of publication

the volume number, in Roman numerals, if you are using a multi-volumed work

the page number or numbers in Arabic numerals, in the following form for a single-volumed work: "p. 92" or "pp. 92–96"; in the following form for a multi-volumed work: "I, 92" or "I, 92–96"

Place a comma between each item in the sequence, except just before the parentheses containing information about place and date of publication. Place a period at the end of the note.

Consider the following examples:

[1]Samuel R. Levin, *The Semantics of Metaphor* (Baltimore: Johns Hopkins University Press, 1977), p. 92.

[2]Paul Ricoeur, "Metaphor and the New Rhetoric," *The Rule of Metaphor: Multidisciplinary Studies of the Creation of Meaning in Language,* trans. Robert Czerny with Kathleen McLaughlin and John Costello (Toronto and Buffalo: University of Toronto Press, 1977), pp. 134–172.

For footnote or endnote references to an article in a periodical, use the following standard format:

the author's name, first name first

the title of the article or essay, in quotation marks

the name of the periodical, underlined or italicized

163

the volume number, in Arabic numerals, followed by a colon and the issue number, if any, in Arabic numerals

in parentheses, the date of the issue

the page number(s) in Arabic numerals

Place a comma between each item in the sequence, except just before the parentheses containing information about place and date of publication. Place a period at the end of the note.

Consider the following example:

[3]Thomas A. Green and W. J. Pepicello, "The Riddle Process," *Journal of American Folklore*, 97:384 (April–June, 1984), 189–203.

At the end of the essay (following the endnotes, if any), provide a bibliography, or alphabetic list of works cited. Use the format above, except that:

the author, or primary author in the case of a work with multiple authors, is given last name first; the names of co-authors are given first name first

a period, rather than a comma, separates the name of the author from the title of the work and the title of the work from the publication data

no parentheses enclose the publication data

page references are eliminated for books, but retained to identify essays collected in books or articles in periodicals

Consider the following examples:

Green, Thomas A. and W. J. Pepicello. "The Riddle Process." *Journal of American Folklore,* 97:384 (April–June, 1984), 189–203.

Levin, Samuel R. *The Semantics of Metaphor.* Baltimore: Johns Hopkins University Press, 1977.

Ricoeur, Paul. "Metaphor and the New Rhetoric." In *The Rule of Metaphor: Multidisciplinary Studies of the Creation of Meaning in Language.* Trans. Robert Czerny with Kathleen McLaughlin and John Costello. Toronto and Buffalo: University of Toronto Press, 1977, pp. 134–172.

Forms of Documentation in the Social and Natural Sciences

The system of documentation now used in publications in the social and natural sciences—and coming into use in some humanities fields—has the advantage of being free from footnotes. This system places brief references in parentheses within the text itself and arranges complete bibliographic information in a list at the end of the text.

The parenthetical references provide the author's last name, the date of publication, and, where necessary, page number, unless that information has already been indicated in the text itself. Consider the following examples:

> Behavioral approaches to the study of metaphor have challenged the notion that there is a special role for metaphor in scientific discovery (Cornwell and Hobbs, 1984).

> Cornwell and Hobbs (1984) have challenged the notion that there is a special role for metaphor in scientific discovery.

At the end of the essay you must provide a bibliography of works cited. Use the following standard format for books and essays collected in a book:

> the name of the author(s), last name first, followed by first and middle initials, ending with a period

> the title of the section of the book, if relevant, without quotation marks, with only the first word of the

title and proper names capitalized, ending with a
period

the name of the editor(s), first and middle initials
first, followed by last name and (Ed.) or (Eds.), ending with a comma

the title of the book, underlined or italicized, with
only the first word of the title and proper names
capitalized, ending with a period

city of publication, followed by a colon

the name of the publisher, followed by a comma

the year of publication, followed by a period

for an essay collected in a book, the page numbers,
in Arabic numerals, preceded by "Pp." and followed by a period

Consider the following examples:

Gerhart, M. and Russell, A. M. *Metaphoric process:
the creation of scientific and religious understanding.*
Fort Worth: Texas Christian University Press, 1984.

Searle, J. R. Metaphor. In A. Ortony (Ed.),
Metaphor and thought. Cambridge and New York:
Cambridge University Press, 1979, Pp. 92–123.

For articles in a journal, use the following standard
format:

the name of the author(s), last name first, followed
by first and middle initials, ending with a period

the title of the article, without quotation marks,
with only the first word of the title and proper
names capitalized, ending with a period

the title of the journal, underlined or italicized, with
all major words capitalized, ending with a comma

publication date, followed by a comma

the volume number, in Arabic numerals, underlined or italicized, followed by a comma

the page numbers included, in Arabic numerals,
ending with a period

Consider the following example:

Cornwell, D. and Hobbs, S. Behavioral analysis of
metaphor. *Psychological Record*, 1984, *34*, 325–332.

Before submitting your manuscript, ask your editor
or instructor what system of documentation you are expected to conform to, and ask for the name of the manual
of style in which that system is fully laid out. Whatever
system you use, be consistent and be complete.

Index

1   2   3   4   5   6   7   8   9   0